# Letters to a
# Writer of Color

*Edited by*
*Deepa Anappara and Taymour Soomro*

Random House
New York

Published in the United States by Random House, an imprint and
division of Penguin Random House LLC, New York.

RANDOM HOUSE and the HOUSE colophon are registered trademarks
of Penguin Random House LLC. Published in the United Kingdom
by Vintage, a division of Penguin Random House UK.

"On the Inactive Protagonist" by Vida Cruz-Borja first printed by
*Fantasy Magazine* in Issue 70 (2021) under the title "We Are the
Mountain: A Look at the Inactive Protagonist"

"On the Second Person" by Kiese Laymon was first printed in *Guernica* on
June 17, 2013, with the title "You Are the Second Person"

Trade paperback ISBN 9780593449417
Ebook ISBN 9780593449424

Printed in the United States of America on acid-free paper

randomhousebooks.com

2 4 6 8 9 7 5 3 1

First U.S. Edition

*Book design by Virginia Norey*

# Contents

# Letters to a Writer of Color

# Introduction

We, the editors of this anthology, are from two nations that were once part of the same country but since independence from British rule, and subsequent partition, have fought multiple wars with each other. Our personal experiences and our backgrounds couldn't be more different. But as students of creative writing, we quickly discovered that we faced similar challenges in an overwhelmingly white classroom, where our writing was measured by a metric that didn't allow for cultural, regional, and racial variance. Fiction that didn't conform to established norms was often rejected as "badly written" or lacking in tension or conflict, without the acknowledgment that these sensibilities had been shaped by, among other things, the white, mostly male aesthetic of the creative writing program itself.

Our own discussions on fiction, therefore, weren't only about elements of a narrative such as voice, character, and plot—subjects that have been examined at length in many writing manuals—but the ways in which race and culture intersected with those tenets of good writing that privileged a Western perspective. These conversations continued as we began to publish our writing and found that our work wasn't always received on the same terms as that of our white counterparts. Readers and reviewers often shelved our fiction under such curious categories as "cultural interest" or "Asia," as if we were not novelists but ethnographers or anthropologists. We were asked more questions about the state of our nations than our writing. A single character's experience was often conflated with the experiences of an entire nationality or community.

Across the world, there is now an understanding of the racial and cultural biases in various bodies of knowledge such as history, medicine, and art and an awareness that we should make space in these epistemologies for women, people of color, LGBTQ+ people, and the working class. What if we similarly reevaluated the codes and conventions that over time have molded our assumptions about how fiction should be written? What form would a more in-clusive approach to storytelling traditions take? How could we challenge popular writing maxims that may not be in keeping with our cultural ethos? How did writers of color center their lived expe-riences, race, and culture in their fiction? The following seventeen essays begin to suggest answers to these questions.

In these pages writers reflect on the shifting shapes of a narra-tive; characters rooted in realisms other than psychological real-ism; the act of translation inherent in writing in English when the action is taking place in a different language; writing queerness, vi-olence, and trauma without stereotyping our communities or shoehorning them into, say, an English or American value system; diktats such as "show, don't tell"; and the importance of characters labeled as inactive in science fiction and fantasy. The essays ask if drawing inspiration from the works of other writers makes our writing any less authentic; if we can write humor when we are expected to represent our country and culture; and if a crime novel set in the non-Western world can provide social and historical context without losing narrative urgency.

Beyond craft, the anthology also examines the writing life because, for us, the question of how to write is inextricable from the question of how to be a writer in the world. The essays suggest how we can combine our art and our activism; respond to readers, editors, and censors; and find resilience. They explore the stories we tell ourselves about who we are as writers and investigate the myth and reality of finding the perfect conditions to write. None of these essays are prescriptive. Rather, they emphasize that no one rule can be considered universal or pertinent to all lives and experiences. More than a craft manual, the anthology is, therefore, a record of each contributor's particular experience of writing and publishing their work.

It is also a book for readers. By broadening and complicating the notion of good writing and by demonstrating its cultural and racial determinants, the essays ask readers to be inclusive not only in *what* they read but *how* they read. We believe the anthology offers readers a new vocabulary to discuss fiction with others.

We recognize that taxonomies such as the "of color" of the anthology's title can be reductive, flattening diverse histories and peoples into an apparently homogeneous cohort, but the essays that follow reflect the multiplicity of our selves. Our hope for this anthology is that it will create a sense of community for readers and writers who feel isolated, misread, silenced, or erased because they do not see their stories on bookshelves or their bodies in fiction.

These essays continue a conversation that other writers of color have begun about the whiteness of English-language fiction and the disservice it does to readers and writers. We need more stories from more cultures, races, communities, and nations to dismantle structures that suppress difference and to challenge the perception that difference is failure. This book is not, and shouldn't be, the last word on the subject.

—*Deepa Anappara and Taymour Soomro*

# On Origin Stories

*Taymour Soomro*

**I collect stories about con artists.** Often the stories stress what is purely, willfully manipulative in the con and its pursuit of simple financial gain, but what interests me more is the desire for a disguise, its art and effects.

Tom MacMaster, a cis-het white American, blogged as a Syrian lesbian. Sophie Hingst posed as the relative of Auschwitz survivors and sent "testimonies" of people who had never existed to Israel's Yad Vashem memorial. Belle Gibson, a wellness guru, claimed to have survived various cancers. Hargobind Tahilramani masqueraded as film studio executive Amy Pascal. And there's Rachel Dolezal, Anna Delvey, and Dan Mallory too. There is a public fascination with uncovering these cons, with unmasking a "true" identity underneath, with pathologizing these acts as sickness or crime.

But I feel a kind of affinity, perhaps even an uneasy kinship, with these actors. My identity seems to me unavoidably a performance and a disguise, not only because it seeks to constrain me in one persona when I am constantly in flux but also because there has always been a conflict between who I think I am at any given moment and who others think I am, so that my reflection flickers endlessly in a mirror. One of the features that distinguishes good fiction for me is that it captures this shiftiness of self, so that Anna Karenina or Rahel Ipe or Sethe cannot be constrained within a fixed identity, cannot easily be reduced to a set of character traits. I wonder then at the relationship between the stories I tell about myself and the stories I write. Where is the con and where is the truth?

These questions recur in Nabokov's formulation on fiction in *Lectures on Literature*: "Literature was born on the day when a boy came crying wolf, wolf and there was no wolf behind him. . . . Between the wolf in the tall grass and the wolf in the tall story there is a shimmering go-between. That go-between, that prism, is the art of literature." For him, fiction is a commitment to untruth rather than truth. It is the ultimate, unimpeachable con.

When I left my job at a corporate law firm to write a novel, my greatest preoccupation was not that I would fail but that my fiction would unmask me. I was living a sort of double life at the time: queer in London but not in Karachi, desi in Karachi but as English as possible in London. This kind of life—of multiple selves, of one person in my head and another outside, of one person in one place and another elsewhere—was familiar to me. It was how I'd always been, but my ability to police these selves, to keep them separate, to keep separate the communities that knew me as one person and those that knew me as another, had become more difficult, once I left home at eighteen for university and began to live these lives rather than just to imagine them.

So when I sat down to write, I determined to write as far away from these selves as I could, "as though tossing a grenade," as the protagonist of my novel *Other Names for Love* says. To support myself, I tutored the children of wealthy Londoners. One of these was a young woman who had enrolled in a graduate program. First, I guided her through the writing process for a thesis on beauty myths and, when she did well on that, through the writing process for a subsequent thesis on the ethics of face transplantation.

My student preferred that we should read and make notes together and, as this was on the clock, it suited me. I spent hours in her Knightsbridge basement apartment reading aloud to her from articles and textbooks, dictating notes, interrupted occasionally by her mother, who would turn up with wads of fifty-pound notes to pay me, and her handsome Cypriot boyfriend, who, when he wasn't napping, drifted in and out of the living room in a short toweling robe which promised at any moment, if I paid sufficient attention, to reveal a glimpse of the inside of his thigh.

I was in search of a protagonist and a plot for my novel. My student, with her ennui, anxiety, and careless wealth, seemed like a character I could imagine piloting the kind of novels I'd read, and the subject matter of her thesis seemed topical and arbitrary enough that none of it could say anything about me at all: the perfect Keyser Söze. Over the two years that I taught her, I wrote, polishing and repolishing the first part of the manuscript. I bought that year's edition of a guidebook called *The Writers' & Artists' Yearbook*, which included an alphabetical list of British agents with brief descriptions, and sent three chapters and a cover letter to a selection of nine agents, who, within a couple of months, rejected the material in standard form.

Thinking back, I can't imagine there could have been any other outcome, but at the time it was startling, so humiliating I couldn't speak of it or think of it or write anymore, ever again. I left London for the safety and security of my parents' home in Karachi. And then, at a loss for what to do and desperate to feel useful, I took over the family farm. I grappled with who I was and who I wanted to be and finally, after coming out to my parents, integrated more coherently the separate selves I had constructed—so that I no longer had to make such careful and fearful decisions about which self I'd be in any given context. I moved back to London. A little humbler, with lower expectations, I thought I'd try writing again. I enrolled in a writing program. I wrote more freely than before, as close to myself as I wanted, no longer throwing a grenade. I began to publish my work, which now frequently featured queer brown characters doing things in Pakistan.

On a recent occasion, I found myself telling this story to a group of students. You see, I told them, I could write truthfully once I lived truthfully. But it's fiction, one of the students said. Yes, I said. It's fiction, but fiction has to be truthful, and once I was true to myself, I could write truthfully, and I realized as I said all this, repeating *true* and *truthful* again and again, trying with the repetition to persuade all of us, that this relationship between truth and fiction didn't really make sense. This origin story, though it had satisfied me and seemed to satisfy others, though it articulated a voguish value system, by celebrating identity, coming out, self-love, self-actualization, though it provided a teachable moment, a craft lesson, was a con, was a wolf shimmering in the tall grass.

Where had it come from? And what was it doing?

It celebrated a particular way of being, of being a good queer, a good immigrant; worse, by endorsing a true identity for me, by drawing a link between that true identity and craft, it suggested in a sly way that my identity is the story I should tell, that *queer immigrant* is the lane my fiction belongs in.

The fiction of mine that has been most successful with industry gatekeepers is fiction that stays in my lane. But on my writing program, I studied with three cis-het white men for whom there seemed to be no lane at all, none that constrained them at least. One of them was writing a novel with a Japanese protagonist, another with an Iraqi, a third a Chinese. Their novels were published soon after we finished our degrees. Their writing and their success unsettled, even irritated me. Was it jealousy? It *was* a kind of jealousy, that they were allowed to, that they had the audacity to tell any story they wanted, as far from their lives, with protagonists as different from themselves as they could possibly be.

It made me wonder whether the power a writer has over their fiction is a power the writer has over their person. The imperative to stay in your lane, to write what you know, these are forces I think many writers must guard against, though some—those who are queer, those who are racialized—seem to be more vulnerable and more sensitive to its effects. The gatekeepers and the readers are not so easily conned by us, so that Elena Ferrante is presumed to be Lenù in her Neapolitan Quartet, so that Monica Ali is presumed to write well only when she writes about Bangladeshi immigrants.

By writing freely, each of the three men I studied with reminded me I had less power than he did, that his fiction, his person was not constrained in the way that I was.

* * *

So, if my origin story is a con, are there are other stories I can tell about my origins as a writer? Or, if fiction is a con, are there other cons that can tell more about how and why I write?

Here is another con. When I was a child, we moved every few years from one country to another, as my father's job required. When I was ten, we moved from Riyadh to Istanbul. I studied, as I had before, at an international school. In each year, there was a single small class with students from all over the world—Indonesia, South Korea, Egypt, Colombia, the Philippines, and elsewhere—and I was at an age when learning was still allowed to be fun. It would have been an idyllic life—a grand house with a ballroom overlooking the Bosphorus, a coop of rowdy chickens in the garden, a pretty pool we never used as none of us could swim—had I not begun in those days to have uncontrollable, unspeakable desires for boys, desires that kept me feverish, tossing and turning through the night. Once, when one of my crushes, a brutish schoolfriend I'll call "F" was at my house for a sleepover, I made a pass at him, ferreting my hand under the covers and onto his stomach. He casually, wordlessly removed my hand and continued the conversation we were having. He didn't speak of it afterward to me or, to my knowledge, to anyone else, and somehow I didn't worry that he would.

I replayed the scenario in my head over and over again. I imagined our roles were reversed, that F had wanted me desperately, that he had acted on his urges. The fantasy thrilled me so much I wrote it out in a letter to a friend in Karachi, telling him about it as though it were true. And then I told another schoolfriend in Istanbul, swearing him to secrecy. We discussed at length F's behavior, what precisely he had done, what it meant, the fantasy gaining the satisfying heft of truth with each conversation. The friend promptly told others in our class, and I was summoned to repeat the story, which I did now with increasing worry. As a result of the gossip, F was shunned by the group. Shortly after, to my relief, we moved to London, but the fear continued to haunt me that I would be found out. Even after I went to college, the feeling of being found out as I imagined it was incomprehensibly terrible to me.

More than a decade after I had left Istanbul, emerging from the changing room of an esoteric boutique off Carnaby Street, I bumped into an old schoolfriend from those days. We caught up on the intervening years. Finally, she asked, did I remember that story I'd told about F? I did. She pressed her lips together and nodded as if to say, how desperately, how uncontrollably you must have wanted him, and though my desires were no longer so unspeakable, I still felt the familiar shiver of humiliation run through me.

It was a con. It was an exercise in storytelling. That sounds callous. Poor F was the victim of my fun and games in fiction. In my defense, the world-building fiction can do, perhaps some of us must do it to build a world in which there is space for us and our desires. The world my story conjured around me was one in which queerness was real, in which I was desirable—the story allowed me to imagine unspeakable parts of myself into existence. But I learned, too, the dangers of a con—the risk not only that my deceit would be found out but that my desires would be found out, and by my desires, I would be unmasked entirely. After all, for a queer person, it can seem as though our desires are what define us and diminish us.

Another con. Throughout my childhood, I would spend summers and winters in Pakistan visiting my parents' families. With my maternal cousins, I'd write and perform little skits for the rest of the family, casting myself invariably as the comical female lead. With my paternal grandfather, who was in those years in and out of government, I'd travel around the country, accompanying him to meet officials, generals, ministers, members of the opposition, where he would introduce me as his "son and heir" and ask me to say something clever.

On one occasion, my grandfather and I stopped unexpectedly in the city where some cousins lived. I hatched a plan to trick one of my cousins by pretending to be a female friend of his sister. I cloaked myself in a shawl so that only my eyes were visible. When he came home from school, I rushed past him and locked myself in his bathroom. Through the closed door I explained that I had been horribly disfigured and was too ashamed to show my face. He sat by the door, comforting me, assuring me that he wouldn't judge me. I was thrilled at the magic that made me into someone else, someone dramatic and captivating, and when I finally revealed myself, I delighted at that as well, because it showed him what a magician I was. My grandfather collected me from the house shortly after so that we could continue on our way, and I told him the clever trick I'd played. "But," he said irritably, "why a girl?" His question and its tone stopped me short. Why, I wondered too, in a way I hadn't before, with a shame I didn't quite understand. Why a girl? Why a girl soliciting attention from a boy? Why a girl ashamed of revealing herself for fear of judgment?

This is the truth in fiction that often fact alone cannot tell—because we don't know our own desires, because we might not admit them to ourselves. When I think of Tom MacMaster, of Sophie Hingst, of Hargobind Tahilramani, of the boy who cried wolf, I wonder at their desires, not only of why they conned, but why *that* con.

But here too was the power of fiction, that another self could shimmer in place of me.

When I was thirteen, my family moved to London. Till then, I had had little sense of what it meant to be Pakistani other than that I spent most holidays in Karachi and Lahore; that on Eid, I wore a salwar kurta when I went to the mosque with my father; that occasionally we spoke Urdu.

I enrolled in a school quite different from those I had studied at before. Learning was no longer to be fun. The school was single-sex, we wore uniforms, and we called our teachers "Sir" and "Miss." All the boys but me spoke alike, cut their hair alike, wore the same jackets and shoes, lived in the same suburbs of London—Chigwell, Woodford, Finchley—places I didn't know. I was alone in my differ-ence, and to be different meant being wrong in a way that was unfa-miliar to me, my wrongness constellating somehow around the way that I was Pakistani.

I had already begun to feel awkward about my voice. I was often misgendered on the telephone—each instance triggering a sense of failure. In London, I grew to hate my voice. Schoolmates would re-peat things I said in a comical accent, and as a result I spoke only when I had to. I practiced softening my consonants, articulating my t's and r's with the tip of my tongue, shortening my vowels, so that I should sound like the others.

I parted my hair in the center; I wore the same black down jacket with orange lining, the same lace-up shoes with steel toe caps. I avoided the kitchen when my mother was cooking so I wouldn't smell of cumin and frying oil. I discouraged my mother from dropping me off at school, so that schoolmates shouldn't see her in a salwar kameez. And when my parents attended events or meetings there, I'd insist they wear Western clothes.

This was a different kind of con, a different kind of story about myself, but no less magical: assimilation as an invisibility cloak, to make me something else.

When I got to college, I started flirting with boys and dressing in a way that caused me frequently to be misgendered, to be stopped at public restrooms, to be cat-called, to be cross-examined on my body and its desires. Did I want to be a woman? But look at the hair on my arms and legs. And what was between them? It embarrassed me. It's only what I like, I said. It doesn't mean anything.

In my final year, two popular athletes at college had a twenty-first birthday party to which I was not invited. I turned up regardless, a little merry, and flirted with a guest from out of town. He was in the army, and we talked about the laws against gays in the military. He'd fight anyone, he said vehemently, who'd stop me from serving, though I had no interest in it at all. We talked and kissed and then I moved on to another venue. In the early hours of the morning, I returned in search of fun and instead found the place somber, the remaining guests stern and tense. Immediately upon seeing me, one of the hosts hustled me out by the arm.

I woke the next day, bleary-eyed, to discover that I was the talk of the college. The man I'd kissed had thought I was a girl, so the story went. On finding out the truth, he'd become wild with fury, gone out in search of me to do who knew what. He was engaged, for God's sake. That wasn't what had happened, I argued, it couldn't have been, he knew exactly who I was—but my friends were disapproving, and in the end even I wondered. I felt humiliated—as though my body were a lie, as though my desirability were a lie. It was easier to believe in queer, colored me as a trickster than the alternative: that desire and sexuality are complex, that queerness is everywhere, that a person cannot be contained by a single story about their body and its wants.

The gift of queerness, of being racialized is, it seems to me, a red pill/blue pill clarity that makes plain the constructedness of truth and identity, because the stories we and others tell about our bodies and their meanings are often so ill-fitting. And of course, these multiple stories conflict, and the conflict makes them unstable, ephemeral. Am I this or that? Am I what you say or what I say? So that our image flickers—in the mirror and to others—and one day we look one way, and another, another way. And as a result, we see in identity its multiplicity, its slipperiness, its shiftiness, that it changes across time and place, that we can change it. I suppose I am suggesting that fiction and a self might be made out of the same material, might be as ephemeral or as real, that autonomy over the self can extend to fiction, that autonomy over fiction can extend to the self.

In my first novel, inspired by my wealthy, anxious student, I wrote far away from myself not only because I was afraid of exposing myself but also because I thought I had no value, because I thought what was far away from me was valuable. I could only write about queerness and Pakistan once those aspects of my identity had some worth for me, and I had to unlearn so much that the world had taught me in order to appreciate their value in my self and my fiction. I am glad I value those aspects of myself; I am glad I write about them so that others should see their value.

At the same time, I find in myself a desire for my fiction to do more than unmask me; I want it to remake me, in the way that a con artist remakes their own image with their story. To resist simple narrow static definitions of who I am is to resist simple narrow definitions of what my fiction can be.

And what is my origin story if not the story I began with? I am everywhere in each of my fictions, as present in *Other Names for Love*, with its young, queer, Pakistani protagonist, as I am in my skits, in my cons, in the novel that failed. The facts of a story may correspond, or not, to the facts of my life, but the story will hold more meaningful truths, obsessions or interests, hurts or loves I can perhaps only tell aslant. "A Sublime Port," a story about a eunuch in sixteenth-century Constantinople, is in part about my failed masculinity. "S&M," a story about an ex who liked to be humiliated in bed, is about *my* attraction to destructive relationships. My novel about face transplantation is about *my* struggles with identity, with a sense of a schism in my identity, of wearing a mask over my face. The failure of that novel is not because I was absent from it. Perhaps it failed because I was too present. Perhaps its plotlessness was the plotlessness of my life. Perhaps its protagonist was as passive as I felt, stymied by the uncertainty of who I was and what I wanted.

Resistance isn't easy—the simple narratives are persuasive so that we must work hard, harder in our fiction to make a reader believe a story that deviates from the stories told about us. For any writer who wishes to publish, the incentives are great to write the story that makes the reader, the editor, the agent, the prize committee comfortable, that endorses their way of seeing the world, that celebrates their values. But this kind of conformity feels, to me, like the kind of submission, the kind of subservience I have tried to resist in relation to my self all my life. And the feeling of fraudulence, the feeling I have now as I write this essay, that I am no writer at all, perhaps that is how resistance feels.

I feel ill-equipped to give any advice to you about how to write— but I am certain of this. When the stories about who you are that you tell, that others tell, become fixed and unchanging, resist, resist, resist—even if you have no more power than to resist in your mind—because your fiction can only be as complex, as dynamic as you allow yourself to be.

*(Some of the names and identifying details in this essay have been changed to protect the privacy of the people involved.)*

## Reading Suggestions

Lesley Nneka Arimah, "Who Will Greet You at Home"
Vikram Chandra, *Love and Longing in Bombay*
Anton Chekhov, *Uncle Vanya*
Ismat Chughtai, "Lihaaf"
Ananda Devi, *Eve Out of Her Ruins*
Romesh Gunesekera, *Reef*
Sterling HolyWhiteMountain, "Featherweight"
Kazuo Ishiguro, *The Remains of the Day*
Uzma Aslam Khan, *The Geometry of God*
Thomas Mann, *Death in Venice*
Daniyal Mueenuddin, *In Other Rooms, Other Wonders*
Madeleine Thien, *Do Not Say We Have Nothing*
Ivan Turgenev, *Fathers and Sons*

# On Structure

*Madeleine Thien*

A composition comes into being as the incarnation
of many living gestures.
—Lu Chi (261–303), *Wen-fu*

The homeland, friends, is a continuous act
As the world is continuous
—Jorge Luis Borges, "Ode Written in 1966"

**I am in Vancouver, and it is early morning, night-dark**. Around me, a circle of high-rises stretches into the sky. Every few moments, the commuter train floats by on a track beneath my window. Soon, its tunneling *whoosh* becomes part of the landscape, and I no longer hear the sound. Light threads the outline of the Cascade Mountains. It is November 17, 2021, and the West Coast is suffering catastrophic rains. Highway One, the only road connecting Vancouver to the rest of Canada, is impassable; thirty minutes from here, towns and cities are covered in water.

The sky is divided in two. The eastern sky is fog and mist, the western sky deep black. Far beyond is the Juan de Fuca Strait and, further still, the islands of my childhood, clustered at the door of the Pacific Ocean. I see fog sitting in gullies of roads and cul-de-sacs, gathering at the knees and hips of swaying pines. Sunrise creeping beneath the fog looks supernatural.

If I think about how to describe the past three days and why I have returned to Vancouver, my eyes water and a heaviness in my chest threatens to stop all movement. So instead I concentrate on the sensory world around me. Through the bedroom door, I can hear my partner, also a writer, talking to himself. His voice is melancholy and fatigued. Talking to oneself might be the novelist's peculiar form of prayer, a way of conversing with characters, with ourselves, and with the half-formed, still forming, book itself. For months and years, we work on books that only we can hear.

Novels are containers whose walls, elusive for the novelist, fold illusively into their surrounding air. They are not constructed from metal, glass, concrete but from patterning and from thought. Even more startling, the character's "thoughts" must emerge from my own experiences or observations, but they are not, in my opinion, my own. Characters show me how they see, and I am tethered to their currents of feeling and sense-making. My thinking happens within the structure, patterning and making, in the abstract form— the space—that makes the particular time and cadence of each novel possible. After two decades of writing, I am never lonely. My characters live in the same apartments and temporary rooms as I do. They go about their business. This helps me do my work. I am not the beginning or end of their existence, just a stranger with whom they struck up a conversation in the street, and this conversing creates, within me, a world. They know a time before me and beyond me.

Last night, I visited my friend and her family. She is a sister to me.

I last saw her three weeks before the start of the global pan-

demic. She beams when I arrive. When we embrace, she makes little scratching motions on my back, an unusual form of hugging, as
if to awaken my nerves. Such a pleasure in these small scratches.

Her son is kneeling on the carpet, playing. He is four years old
and loves numbers. When he was two, he would fervently tap numbers into phones and calculators, shouting out their names: "One
million two hundred eighty-three thousand four hundred and
sixty-eight!" It was astonishing and a little alarming, his little body
emitting a wonder that no happiness was greater than the happiness of large numbers.

In the living room, he leans, rapt, over hundreds of square tiles,
each the size of a Triscuit. Sevens are green, sixes are orange, zeroes
are red, and so on.

Without realizing I am doing it, I start to organize the pieces by
color. Arrangement gives me a sense of calm. He regards me with
interest and also suspicion. My partner joins the game. He begins to
add and subtract the tiles: six minus two is four, and the three numbers bask in their newfound friendship.

6 2 4

My friend's son is overjoyed. He adds and adds, bringing 147 with
398 to make 545. The nine numbers gaze at us with the content-
ment of a square:

1 4 7
3 9 8
5 4 5

\* \* \*

We rearrange by instinct, color, aesthetics, and a desire to surprise one another. I am suddenly aware, in a wash of memory, of being his age, four years old. It is a regular Saturday night, and the grown-ups are playing mahjong. When they "wash the tiles" it sounds like they're breaking all the dishes in the house. They build the walls that start the game, lift and discard pieces, gossip, tell vulgar jokes, and hunt down the runs, groupings, and triplicates that will make them rich. They play all night. Every Saturday is different, every Saturday is the same. In the morning, we watch cartoons while the adults snooze.

The living room table is alive with sorting, sequencing, and re-configuring.

My friend and I talk. Sometimes she is suffering, and pain creases across her body.

I do not want to hover or make my gaze a burden. But I want to take the pain away, for it is too much for one person to hold.

My friend has been given a devastating prognosis. In the space of a few weeks, so much that seemed ordinary and everyday has unraveled. Life is now a tiny shell of time. We talk about wills, decisions, finances, books, projects, jobs, work, family, motherhood. We face what is known, but we hope for an unknown that defies what medicine foresees. She is young, healthy, and strong. She wants to live. I have never wanted something so much.

My friend has spent more than a decade writing about the Cambodian genocide and about how people remember, forget, survive, succumb, change. The years that I spent writing about the genocide were the most transformative, and also the most devastating, of my life, and I have long worried for her well-being. The two of us have spoken often about the many shapes of forgetting, how the United States could drop 2.7 million tons of bombs on Cambodia, a country with which it was not at war, and entirely forget that it had done so. How, for some who lived through that time, forgetting was, is, the price of survival. My friend has written extensively about my novel, *Dogs at the Perimeter,* focusing on aphasia, neurology, the loss of language, and the channels that develop new communicative forms when language fails.

My friend is a scholar and inhabits a world where people theorize. But she has a further relationship with the responsibility and hope of writing. Her parents and older brothers survived the genocide, and her mother was pregnant when the family, driven one way and another by the pursuing Khmer Rouge, was plucked out, in a chaotic moment, by aid workers. They were permitted to board a bus out of Cambodia and to enter a refugee camp in Thailand. She writes to record, understand, signify, analyze, and contend—to see with greater clarity, which is, ultimately, to love. A small word so often misused or derided.

What is the shape of such a thing? A word so small it seems to fit inside the hand, but so small it always escapes our hold.

I am in the sixth year of working on a novel, which I hope will become my fifth book. I am working with shapes, figures, and patterns, the nontextual expression of a novel, as much as with words. I draw my circle, my sentence, my paragraph and consider it. I draw another line. Certain chapters float, like multiple transparencies, over other chapters. My process is frustratingly slow, but uncertainty gives me a sense of freedom. The first few years of writing usually never appear in my novels. They are sketches, experiments, abandoned beginnings, middles of all kinds: a kind of wandering.

Characters know their world, but I am a newcomer. This process of making and unmaking is crucial for me.

Everywhere I look as I work, simple things flourish into complex things; they grow and change and pass away. The physicist Carlo Rovelli writes that we describe the world as it happens, not as it is: structure is a process, an activity. Where there is movement, there is time. Rovelli observes that time is an aspect of perspective. He says the world is made of events not things and that even the hardest stone is a long event. A stone is "a process that for a brief moment manages to keep its shape, to hold itself in equilibrium before disintegrating again into dust." When I look up from his words, the surfaces around me—book, table, chair, trees, rain—reveal themselves as made out of time, built from it.

Is this not confusing, though, to say that structure is a movement, not a fixity? But this speculation—that things are made of change—is part of all the old philosophies. Liu Xie, writing at the turn of the sixth century, composed a groundbreaking essay on shensi 神思, a term that encompasses thought, imagination, spirit, mind, and feeling. Shensi refers to what is contained within us (intent, thought), and it refers, as well, to the ways in which thinking roams and to mental activity that is fathomless. Various scholars have compared shensi to the Greek daimon, a divide or restlessness that inhabits us and leads us into the unknown. In Chinese usage, shensi is not a form of anguish and is not—as sometimes occurs in usage of daimon or daemon—related to the demonic. Rather, shensi is changeability at its very limits and is associated with inner (mental, emotional, and spiritual) freedom.

*Wenxin diaolong*, Liu Xie's masterpiece, is made of fifty concise essays on literary form and compositional technique. It is, to borrow a phrase from scholar Stephen Owen, "both literature and literary thought." More than fifteen hundred years later, it remains a touchstone of the Chinese literary world. *Wenxin diaolong*, in its detailed examination of the literary canon of its time and its analysis of the philosophy of literary creation, reoriented—for over a thousand years—the poetry and prose forms that followed.

Composition is a process that begins long before any word is set down. Liu Xie describes accurately and movingly what many writers will recognize: the way we travel far from ourselves, the way our thoughts are shaped by sensory experience and things as well as by memory and imagination; the way a writer attempts, with language, to take hold of these recognitions; the ways in which we pattern and structure language in order to bring unity to breadth. Thinking and ideas are developed in a vast realm; writing is confined to a limited space. "There is an inherent difficulty," writes Ronald Egan in a wonderful essay on shensi, "in bridging the gap between the emptiness in which ideas take shape and the realities that words denote." This confined space is where artfulness is forged. How? Liu Xie observed that the writer applies a balance, a weight, a patterning, keeps a kind of "tally." Structure comes into being as a writer threads the slippage between the envisioned and the real; structure must be found. A piece of writing makes the room in which it can exist. "The literary mind," he declared, "is that mind which strives after literary forms."

I would hazard a guess that many writers will find this way of defining structure disorienting. Liu Xie, in fact, spends the first half of *Wenxin diaolong* enumerating and analyzing more than two hundred different forms already in existence and widely used, including humor, lament, prayers, war reportage, letters, speculative texts, and so on. But in the second half of the book, when he turns to the creative act, he is after something of a different order. Existing forms do not create the work; they are measurements, rulers, and guideposts, like the lives lived before us. They help us examine our inheritance and our future. Composition is not memory or reformulation: it is a personal matter. A person's breadth of vision is their own "turning of the mind," and structure is a unity "binding everything by a single thread"—the reasoning of the writer is what gives meaning to the structure. The mind's capacity to see that single thread is as important as its freedom to roam. Liu Xie writes, "The mind responds to reason therein. . . . Ruminations are settled by controlling the tally."

Perhaps what is most exciting to me about *Wenxin diaolong* is that it is a literary map that offers no blueprint for the craft of writing, and it manages to do this in a Chinese literary tradition renowned for its discipline and rules. The concept of shensi, Egan writes, has a "restive variability," and what separates one work from another are the layers of imaginative thinking discovered by each writer. Moreover: forms change. Movements give rise to counter-movements. Liu Xie hammers home this sense of continua: writing maintains an adaptability to the variations of life, and its defining quality is this sensitivity to new modes of expression. In this way, a writer can "drink out of a spring which is inexhaustible." Translator Vincent Shih observes that, for Liu Xie, the "literary forms of each generation conform to the spirit of that generation and, when changes take place in the spirit of the age, literary forms modify themselves accordingly."

Earlier I said that the insights of Liu Xie and his predecessors opened new pathways for literary thinking. Chinese classical novels, argues Franco Moretti, were generated from different "choices that eventually add up to alternative structures." *The Story of the Stone* by Cao Xueqin, also known as *The Dream of the Red Chamber,* covers a dozen years in two thousand pages. In his joyful study of the inventiveness of small- and large-scale symmetries in Chinese novels, Moretti describes "hemispheric movements" in which a gigantic deck of characters is reshuffled: these recombinations create both novelty and deepening insight. ("In the first twenty chapters of the novel," Moretti writes in *Distant Reading,* "Bao-yu speaks to fifty-four characters, and not once does the same group re-form around him.") Narrative movement is not driven by what happens *next*, that is, what lies "ahead" of a given event, but

> what lies "to the side" of it: all the vibrations that ripple across this immense narrative system—and all the *counter-vibrations* that try to keep it stable. . . . In the novel's overall architecture there are blocks of ten, twenty, even fifty chapters that mirror each other across hundreds of pages. . . . It's really an alternative tradition.

I feel a tremendous resonance with these structures. *The Story of the Stone* was the only novel my mother kept on her bookshelf. It was her favorite book, one of the few possessions that she carried the length of her emigration, from Hong Kong to Australia to Malaysia to Canada, and that remained with her until her death forty years later. In the days after her passing, my mother's sisters drew this novel from the bookcase. Because I cannot read Chinese, I had not even recognized that it was a novel. I had never known, in the too brief time we had together, how greatly she had loved and dwelled within the structures of this book.

In time, we witness the endings of people we have known all our waking lives. In the last days of my father's life, he remained in the cardiac emergency ward. They could not move him to palliative care because they feared he might pass away in the space from here to there—in a hallway, elevator, or passageway. My father was not afraid of death, but he wanted me to alleviate his suffering. I begged the nurses to increase his pain medication. "Do you understand what you're asking?" one asked. What did I understand? Only that an ending should not wrench him away from the person— self-reliant, complex, and private—he wished to remain. Endings, too, should have a continuity.

In Yiyun Li's *Where Reasons End*, the chapters are conversations with the narrator's son. He has died, but he reaches her in the time and space of the page. This novel, spare and probing and also etched by humor and wonder, creates an entirely new form: the narrow passageway in which a mother and child can keep contact in the aftermath of suicide. A space of love without answers. "Will the memory paper," the mother writes, "catch words yet to be said?" Near the end of this extraordinary, incendiary novel, mother and son exchange these lines:

> You always say words fall short, he said.
> Words fall short, yes, but sometimes their shadows can
>     reach the unspeakable.

Words don't have shadows, Mommy. They live on the page,
        in a two-dimensional world.
Still, we look for some depth in words when we can't find it
        in the three dimensional world, no?

Such fractal dimensions are, in *Where Reasons End*, a continua-
tion of love by other means—an antechamber, perhaps the only
one, where the dead and the living can coexist, the memory paper
where such communication can find refuge; the novel creates a literary pattern, which is to say, a room, a structure, that can be entered long after we, too, are gone.

Time accumulates, giving things the space to change. The rup-
tures within a work are as integral as the continuities. Detail and
scale continuously shape a writer's decisions: one sentence follows
another, but through patterning of meaning, sound, images, syntax, and concepts, the planes of a novel begin to generate, intersect,
diverge, and reconfigure. Structure is the wordless part of a story.

Mikhail Bakhtin spent decades pondering time and space in the
novel. Examining Dostoevsky and Rabelais, he asked questions
such as: In what kind of space are this novel and these characters
being realized? What is the spatial form of the hero? What is the
temporal form of the protagonist? He says that a novel is made out
of clay, and the story and characters within it are never finalized. A
novel can never contain itself or compartmentalize itself against
the ongoing present, for it is always oriented toward a future answer. The novel, Bakhtin argues, may be a young form, but its lin-
eage can be found in a history of long prose forms. These forms are
indebted to the eternally living element—the transforming clay of

spoken, informal language—which gathers and carves pathways of unofficial thought.

I can't get Bakhtin to stop chattering in my ear. Shall I take over for you, he jokes, and explain what structure *is*? He wears a very big, heavy coat and lights one cigarette after another. Is structure the apparent unity of form, he asks, or is structure, in fact, the loopholes? He describes two people facing one another. He tells me that their horizons, and thus their worlds, will never coincide:

> . . . I shall always see and know something that he, from his place outside and over against me, cannot see himself: parts of his body that are inaccessible to his own gaze (his head, his face, and its expression), the world behind his back, and a whole series of objects and relations, which in any of our encounters are accessible to me but not to him. As we gaze at each other, two different worlds are reflected in the pupils of our eyes.

We cannot see the world, the objects and relations, behind our backs, nor the inner world visible in our faces. In *Art and Answerability,* Bakhtin calls this the "excess of seeing"—forever unavailable to us except through the eyes of another. When you are sitting here, Bakhtin continues, when you stare out at the city of Vancouver, at the fog and mountains, at the atmospheric river, no one else will ever occupy this time-space location, no matter the infinity of the universe. Yet your uniqueness must also consist of the fact that you are forever an outsider to the locations of others.

My friend can see what passes through my eyes, things of which

I am dimly or not at all aware. She is irreplaceable. When we pass from this world, the patterns we perceive, the layers of touch that have formed us, the excess of seeing, nurtured over a lifetime, inherited, fought for, continuously changing, will also pass away.

My friend and I take a walk down to Granville Island. It is a cold November afternoon, a biting wind and a blue sky. The forecast says that heavy rains will return tomorrow and with it the potential for catastrophic flooding. Right now, the angle of the sun is low, its light silver. We talk about the present and the future. She may have a year. She is only forty-one. We talk about how a decade can slip away without a person realizing it, and how a year can hold a lifetime. We cry. The mathematician Benoit Mandelbrot approached the seemingly simple question *How long is a coastline?* with an open and searching mind. He answered that the measurement is infinite. The granular shape never ceases, forever giving rise to crevices and therefore to ever-increasing amounts of space. To novels. The coastline is between dimensions, punctuated by geometric designs, fractals, interstices.

We talk about a story by Borges, "The Secret Miracle," in which a man is sentenced to death by firing squad. He is just past the age of forty: "Apart from a few friendships and many habits, the problematic practice of literature constituted his life." He mourns a play that he will leave unfinished. He begs God for one more year of life. In a dream, he enters a library and finds God embodied in a single letter in the pages of a discarded atlas. A voice tells him: "The time for your work has been granted." The next day, when the order to fire is given to the execution squad, time stops. Smoke from a soldier's cigarette hangs motionless in the air, and a drop of rain sliding down his cheek hangs in suspension. A whole day passes before he understands that he can still think and compose. In his mind, he writes and revises his play. "Meticulous, unmoving, secretive, he wove his lofty invisible labyrinth in time." When the last word is set down, he feels the drop of rain on his cheek begin to move. The *sonorous, sounding* words he has composed linger in his mind. Shots ring out; the man is killed.

While we are talking, light refracts off the glass buildings, the inlet, the balustrades. A large seagull lands on the railing a foot away and passes a gentle half hour staring at us. Boats go by, and when we look west, we can see the inlet giving way to the strait, which flows between the islands and into the Pacific. We are at the end and the beginning. Darkness falls, and we are still talking. It is cold. When I put my arm around her, I feel her fragile shoulders but also the gravity of her existence. Earlier in the day, a woman shouted at us for walking too slowly along the sidewalk. I am normally combative, but I had held my tongue. I don't know whom to fight anymore.

In a handful of hours it will be morning again. We will have grown a little older. Where did that seagull fly away to? Where did the boat go, and the hurrying woman, and the light? The light falling around us is always novel to the earth's atmosphere, having traveled phenomenal distances. If I stop, what will happen? What comes after the end? I dream of my friend all night. I briefly wake and think: let me dream of something else, let my mind journey elsewhere. My mind refuses. When I open my eyes I am still behind myself, trying to hold on to what has passed. I spend the morning reading Bakhtin. He sits across from me, carrying the excess of seeing. Everything overflows its boundaries. He reminds me of the surplus of character that cannot be captured by the page or the novel. He reminds me that structure is in the loopholes. That it is a living, thinking thing. That contemplation is an action, an activity. That structure is the making of a wholeness that must escape its shape. The old Chinese literary texts echo this belief. In the fourth century, Lu Chi wrote, "A composition comes into being as the incarnation of many living gestures." A composition is the form of endless change.

My friend's son kneels on the floor sorting his numbers, colors, and patterns. Every number, every piece held between thumb and finger, hints at infinity and at its own belonging.

## Reading and Other Suggestions

J. S. Bach, The Goldberg Variations
Mikhail Bakhtin, *The Dialogic Imagination*
Mikhail Bakhtin, *Art and Answerability*
Ludwig van Beethoven, Piano Concertos 30, 31, and 32
Jorge Luis Borges, *Ficciones,* translated by Anthony Kerrigan
Dionne Brand, *Love Enough*
Hermann Broch, *The Death of Virgil,* translated by Jean Starr
    Untermeyer
Cai Zong-qi, editor, *A Chinese Literary Mind: Culture, Creativity,*
    *and Rhetoric in Wenxin Diaolong*
Javier Cercas, *Soldiers of Salamis,* translated by Anne McLean
John Coltrane, *A Love Supreme*
Tsitsi Dangarembga, *Nervous Conditions*
Du Fu, *Selected Poems of Tu Fu,* translated by David Hinton

Damon Galgut, *In a Strange Room*

James Gleick, *Chaos*

Rawi Hage, *Beirut Hellfire Society*

Shirley Hazzard, *The Great Fire*

David Hinton, *Hunger Mountain: A Field Guide to Mind and Landscape*

Bohumil Hrabal, *I Served the King of England*, translated by Paul Wilson

Liu Hsieh, *The Literary Mind and the Carving of Dragons,** translated by Vincent Yu-Chung Shih

Ma Jian, *Beijing Coma*, translated by Flora Drew

Yiyun Li, *Where Reasons End*

Bernadette Mayer, *Midwinter Day*

Rohinton Mistry, *A Fine Balance*

Franco Moretti, *Distant Reading*

Toni Morrison, *Jazz*

Alice Munro, *Open Secrets*

Iris Murdoch, *The Sea, the Sea*

Marie NDiaye, *Self-Portrait in Green*, translated by Jordan Stump

* Notes on the two Chinese texts: Liu Hsieh, *The Literary Mind and the Carving of Dragons*, is available with introduction and translation by Vincent Yu-Ching Shih. Liu Xie 劉勰 (Liu Hsieh in the Wade-Giles romanization system) lived from 465 to 522. *Wenxin diaolong*, translated by Shih as *The Literary Mind and the Carving of Dragons*, is sometimes left with the title untranslated, due to the complexity of the literary terms contained within it. Ronald Egan's wonderful essay "Poet, Mind, and World: A Reconsideration of the Shensi Chapter of *Wenxin diaolong*" can be found in *A Chinese Literary Mind: Culture, Creativity and Rhetoric in Wenxin Diaolong*, ed. Zongqi Cai. An annotated translation of Lu Chi's *Wen-fu* can be found in Stephen Owen's illuminating *Readings in Chinese Literary Thought*. Lu Chi 陸機 (Lu Ji in pinyin romanization) lived from 261 to 303.

Yoko Ogawa, *The Memory Police,* translated by
     Stephen Snyder
Michael Ondaatje, *Coming Through Slaughter*
Stephen Owen, *Readings in Chinese Literary Thought*
Rithy Panh, *The Missing Picture*
Carlo Rovelli, *The Order of Time*
Gjertrud Schnackenberg, *Heavenly Questions*
Adania Shibli, *Touch,* translated by Paula Haydar
Y-Dang Troeung, *Landbridge*
Eliot Weinberger, *The Ghosts of Birds*

# On Authenticity

*Amitava Kumar*

1.

**In his novel *The Cocoon*, Bhalchandra Nemade writes** about a five-year-old girl dying from smallpox in a village in Maharashtra. The child's mother says, "Speak, Mani, speak. Tomorrow, you won't be able to speak. Speak to me today." The narrator of Nemade's novel says that the child remains silent. Then, the grandmother says, "Manutai, what shall I ask big brother to fetch you from Poona?" This time the child answers.

"A red sari."

Another day or two later, the child's mouth will not open. She will lose her sight, her eyes turning white like shells.

There are things that you read and are never able to forget. *That* red sari that the brother, who is the hapless, heartbroken narrator, will now never buy for his sister is one of those things. Does it stay alive in my mind because it is authentic? I don't know. The truth is that I can see the red sari in my mind's eye, and I'm in touch with the infinite regret that fills our lives. It is real in my imagination, that red sari.

In Ismat Chughtai's short story "The Wedding Shroud," Kubra's mother is worried about her daughter's wedding; she would like Kubra to marry her nephew, Rahat, who has come to live with their family. Despite their poverty, every morning Kubra prepares a fine breakfast for Rahat; she makes parathas and eggs and keeps the milk on boil "so that a heavy layer of cream forms on it." When Rahat leaves for work, Kubra rushes into his sleeping quarters, and she hears wedding trumpets in her ears as she goes in to "sweep up the dirt in Rahat's room with her lashes." I try to guess the original Urdu phrase that Chughtai must have used. *To sweep up the dirt with her eyelashes.* Such fine hyperbole, so natural to the languages I grew up speaking. Ultimately, Kubra will remain unmarried. In fact, she will soon die. Is it only the sadness that moves me so? No, the story is so powerful for me because all through the years of my youth I knew the faces of young women, mostly my cousins, who were waiting to be married even while they were burdened by a lack of money, and sometimes, it would appear, even by good looks and the way in which the laws of feudal patriarchy kept them locked in their homes. This literature makes my memories feel authentic.

One more quick example. The first line of Arundhati Roy's *The God of Small Things* tells us that the month of May in Ayemenem in Kerala is "a hot, brooding month." A description follows of the effects of heat, a clash of vivid verbs, hard consonants hitting the page. Then the monsoon breaks. With the rain comes change so radical and so widespread that, if you are a reader like me, you submit to the voice. The prose, with its extravagant energy, carries you. That surrender on my part is a recognition of something original and authentic present in the writer's voice.

I'm saying all this in order to make clear that authenticity isn't a single identity card or license that you carry in your wallet. It confers legitimacy, yes, but it isn't singular. It takes varied forms and emerges from the rich resources of language and memory. In this essay, I want to take note of some of its features, and I see these as nothing but thin shards of perception.

## 2.

Authenticity is often an acquired trait; you aren't necessarily born with it. I was sitting in the living room of a house in south Delhi, just a few minutes' walk from Humayun's Tomb in Nizamuddin East. This was in the home of the famous thinker Ashis Nandy. I had finished reading to him the closing pages of a nonfiction book I had just published, *Husband of a Fanatic*. These pages were about a recent meeting with men in Bhagalpur who had been blinded by the police back in 1980 when I was a teenager. I was worried whether I had got it right.

Nandy must have sensed my anxiety. I was born and grew up in Bihar but at that time had been living abroad for nearly two decades. He began telling me that the most authentic portrayal of the Indian countryside, and of the realities of peasant life, is Satyajit Ray's film *Pather Panchali*. But Ray, Nandy wanted me to know, was a thoroughly Westernized urban dweller, a wildly talented cosmopolitan who played the piano and used a knife and fork to eat even the Bengali staple of rice and fish curry. Ray's first genuine encounter with a village only took place when he started shooting his film. Authenticity in art, like everything in art, is born of artifice (from *art-*, *ars* "acquired skill, craftsmanship" + *facere* "to make, bring about, do"). *Pather Panchali* was inspired, in part, by Italian neorealist cinema—as is attested by this cutting from a magazine that has been in one of my writing notebooks for more than a decade and a half:

> On a business trip to London in 1950, Ray watched Vittorio de Sica's 'Bicycle Thieves' more than a dozen times. He wrote the screenplay for 'Pather Panchali' on the ship back home.

3.

The problem of authenticity for me is always one of naming. It is a language problem. I think I became conscious of this when I was sixteen or seventeen. I was attending school in Delhi. It was July, and I was walking on the street after dinner. The sun had set, but the sky still remained bright with a faint orange hue. I remember asking myself how I would describe the lights that had come on over the Safdarjung flyover. And then I saw the giant bats that were slowly beating their wings across the sky. I wondered about this, how a writer would describe this sight, and then a few days later came a revelation.

In class we read a chapter by Khushwant Singh about the village of Mano Majra. I didn't know this at that time, but the chapter was an excerpt from Singh's famous novel *Train to Pakistan*. In the chapter, I came across a passage about the train on its way to Lahore blowing its whistle each day and bringing the village awake in an instant. Crows begin to caw, and the mullah proclaims the call to prayer. And also this: "Bats fly back in long silent relays and begin to quarrel for their perches in the peepul." ("Long silent relays." How extraordinarily simple and exact, that phrasing.) And then, the reversal in the evening when the goods train steams in: "Little bats go flitting about in the dusk and large ones soar with slow graceful sweeps."

I found these descriptions not just accurate but also magical. I told myself that I would become a real writer once I was able to write sentences that described the world around me in such precise and lyrical ways. A little later, I became a student at Delhi's Hindu College but would skip class to go to the Lalit Kala Akademi Library near Mandi House. There, for the first time, I read Ved Mehta. Mehta wrote about his father, a doctor in the Public Health Department in Punjab, and his own schooling in an orphanage-like school for the blind in Bombay. In an English that was plain and unfussy, Mehta made me see that the road outside my house or my relatives in Motihari, not to mention my Punjabi math teacher in Modern School on Barakhamba Road nearby, could all be written about in readable prose—and were therefore real.

Another thing: in Khushwant Singh's chapter about Mano Majra, he had written that crows cawed in the keekar trees. That was the name for the hardy acacia trees that were common also in Delhi. How could one be a writer if one was unable to name the trees in your town? In Delhi's Lodhi Garden, the trees had small metal nametags nailed into their trunks. That is how I learned that the tree outside my father's government quarters in Chanakyapuri was a saptaparni with the botanical name *alstonia scholaris*. The music of that name has stayed with me and, at last, I have put it in a novel.

I now live on a college campus in upstate New York. Like the trees in Lodhi Garden, the trees on campus also have little nametags. Yellowwood, tulip tree, red oak, sugar maple, weeping willow, American chestnut, London planetree, Chinese elm, Japanese zelkova, Alaska cedar, sweetgum, magnolia, flowering dogwood, and many others. During our walks in the evening, I sing out the names of the trees whenever my wife praises their flowers or foliage. She doesn't know this, but I'm making a statement about the landscape I now inhabit. *I belong here. At least a little bit.*

## 4.

My grandmother wasn't literate, but her language was always alive. She spoke a dialect called Bhojpuri, her speech full of metaphors and similes. By the time I started writing seriously I was far from her and then she was gone. However, the color and immediacy of her phrases have stayed with me. Once she told me that if I came back to India with a white girl, it was going to be difficult. Why? This imaginary white partner of mine, she said, would find her ugly. But why? Because, my grandmother said bashfully, her nose was as flat as bedbug's back.

That's another measure of authenticity—can you spin in language the relationship between things? You announce your comfort in a language when you use imagery, especially for the purpose of comedy. After my grandmother died, I put her nose in the novel I was then writing.

I wish I had talked to my grandmother and asked her questions. She had lived through what came to be called the Spanish flu and then the great Nepal-India earthquake of 1934, not to mention the man-made historical cataclysms of the Bengal Famine and then the horrible bloodbath of Partition in 1947. How would her imagery announce itself and also shift as she described these vast social up-heavals?

One way to judge authenticity is by the purity of the voice. But again, "purity" is the wrong word. The most compelling voice in non-fiction is also the richest and most enduring fabrication: the inter-views collected and given shape by Svetlana Alexievich. I have taught *Voices from Chernobyl* a handful of times in my journalism class. The stories that people tell in the book are vivid, surprising, and utterly shattering. Alexievich has said that she isn't interested in readers be-cause readers can only offer banalities. But her interviewees, who are after all not that removed from her readers, never offer banalities. How does Alexievich collect these startling testimonials? It takes an enormous artistic effort to create such authenticity: for *Voices from Chernobyl*, over a long period exceeding ten years, Alexievich con-ducted more than 500 interviews from which she chose 107, which is to say one in five. Each interview took up four or more tapes, result-ing in about 100 to 150 printed pages, of which only 10 or so pages would finally remain. After she won the Nobel, I read that Alexievich had found her voice by emulating her fellow Belarusian writer Ales Adamovich, who created a genre which he variously described as "the collective novel," "novel oratorio," "novel-evidence," "people talking about themselves," and "epic chorus." In another interview, Alexievich said, "I had no desire at all to work with traditional genres, because if I choose those, in that moment the lucidity, the authentic-ity is lost. That's why I feel that in our times the witness and literature itself are the protagonists." Alexievich was also quoted as saying that this novel with voices was the result of a search for "a literary method that would allow the closest possible approximation to real life." Life becoming authentic by being turned into literature.

5.

Is your sense of the authentic rooted in what is old? Or unchanging, and maybe even atavistic? I can assume that the sounds of a partic- ular chant or sacred prayer plays that role in someone's imagina- tion. In my case, the stink of the bathrooms in the second-class compartments on a train like the Magadh Express is immediately recognizable as real. It is the smell of shit but also something sharper and ammoniac, urine certainly, and maybe also a closed stale feeling of claustrophobic despair. That stink possesses for me the singular, shattering force of degree zero truth. The challenge is to find a debased language adequate to its representation and to keep reinventing the language when returning to a reality that doesn't change for me.

More can be added to the above list: my dead mother's voice, preserved on my answering machine; Premchand's stories in the original Hindi; Vinod Kumar Shukla's stories, even when translated into English; the dead air in the waiting rooms of hospitals and clin- ics in my hometown, Patna; a bowl of perfectly made dal in a road- side dhaba in the middle of nowhere in north India; the boredom of weddings delayed by several hours in the middle of summer in rural Bihar, the thin men in shabby red uniforms with gold brocade wait- ing beside their band instruments.

6.

When I came to the U.S. from India, I wrote nothing about my life in the new country for many years. On the first page of my novel *Immigrant, Montana,* my narrator Kailash says, "To those who welcomed me to America, I wanted to say, without being asked, that *E.T.* ought to have won the Oscar over *Gandhi*. I had found the latter insufficiently authentic but more crucially I felt insufficiently authentic myself." Kailash feels he lacks a "suitable narrative" to present to the people he is meeting. What is a "suitable narrative"? If you will allow that *Immigrant, Montana* was such an account, a "suitable narrative" as far as I was concerned, then it took me thirty years to shape it. In other words, the sense of a coherent narrative cannot be instantly conjured or arrived at effortlessly. I had published books before, but it was at the end of a long journey that I was able to find a voice that was at once fictional, inventive, and playful while also rooted in what could be called reportage, travelogue, memoir. I couldn't have done this earlier. During my early days as a new immigrant on a student visa, I would sit in the basement of the university library and read Mahasweta Devi's writings in the journal *Economic and Political Weekly*. Devi was famous as a prose writer and also a playwright, but these pieces were more like testimonials. They were brief dispatches on the conditions of Adivasi life, offering snapshots on the oppression but, as important, the resistance of the indigenous peoples in places like Jharkhand, where I had spent a part of my childhood. The published copy—no glossies or photographs—was simple but serious. If memory serves, Devi had written in one of these pieces that the Indian writer must have the dust of the villages between their toes. That was one recipe for acquiring authenticity, and I accepted it as an instruction.

On my first trip back to India on a research scholarship, I traveled to Calcutta to meet Devi. And then I went to Jharkhand to interview Adivasi activists. At the end of the visit, I wrote a column for *The Times of India* pompously titled "Intellectuals Must Come

Out of the Shadow of the State." It would take many years and a great deal of travel and research, not least a visit to Bastar to meet the Adivasi activist Soni Sori, before I could tell myself that I had produced a report of the kind that might have pleased Mahasweta Devi. Entitled "The Fall of a Sparrow," it is a part of my novel *A Time Outside This Time,* a report on a killing in which the state plays the role of the producer of bad fiction. At the time I had written it, the op-ed about intellectuals and the state had seemed entirely adequate and even authentic; in giving substance and narrative form to another story in "The Fall of a Sparrow," I was trying to achieve what seemed authentic at this historical moment. "The Fall of a Sparrow" could not have been written without the encounters I had in Jharkhand and Chhattisgarh; on the other hand, it wasn't just the experience that lent authenticity to my writing. No, what was also necessary was artistic distance.

7.

Just the other day, I was writing about a man buying a cigarette at a kiosk in a small town in Bihar. He had bought the cigarette and was then lighting it from a thin rope that dangled, one end smoldering, from a nail driven into a tree. The wording wasn't quite right, and I was trying to remember where I had read a more accurate description in the past. And then it came to me. In V. S. Naipaul's *India: A Million Mutinies Now,* the writer describes walking to Dadar railway station in Bombay: "Outside the vegetable market, where the smells were high, boys were lifting wet vegetable rubbish with their bare hands into Ashok Leyland garbage-compacting trucks." And then there was the line I was looking for: "Dadar station—with its high, gloomy platforms, its crowd, the echoing sound of the crowd, the stalls, the shoeshine boys and men, the twist of the slow-burning rope tied to a metal pillar for people to light their cigarettes from— gave a feel of the big city: as though trains and the constant movement of people had the power, by themselves, to generate excitement." How precise this writing is! The long sentence is as crowded as a train station, but the words and the details they describe are as organized as the cars attached to each other on a train. We start at one place and by the end of the sentence we have arrived in a new one.

Naipaul's powers of observation are exemplary. Many years ago, when I first met the writer Akhil Sharma in New York City, I had a question for him. Sharma had left India when he was a small boy. He had grown up in New Jersey and had gone to elite colleges in the U.S., and yet, in his debut novel, *An Obedient Father,* he presented an intimate portrait of a corrupt official in the Education Department in Delhi. How had he managed to do this?

Sharma said that one of the books that had inspired him was Naipaul's *India: A Million Mutinies Now.* From Naipaul he had learned how to look.

I wanted to confirm that I had remembered this correctly. The interview I had done had taken place more than twenty years ago. When I wrote to Sharma to confirm my memory, he sent me this response:

> What the book taught me was not so much to look as to look again. There are a number of times in the book where Naipaul compares how he sees something with how he saw it decades ago. This layering taught me that even perhaps

the most acute observer of 20th century literature consistently misinterpreted important things because of his anxiety. Now, when I look at something, I look at it and then ask myself what this would look like for someone who isn't afraid.

## 8.

In a piece of fiction I'm working on right now, an Indian woman who is a reporter for CNN in Atlanta has this memory:

> I had become conscious that when we were in the company of educated people in Patna, my father would tell them that he was born in the same hospital as Orwell in Motihari. I later found out that Orwell was indeed born in the same sleepy town as my father, close to our ancestral village Khewali, but it is quite likely that his mother had given birth in the small bungalow that served as the Orwell residence. Richard Blair, Orwell's father, was a sub-deputy opium agent for the British. The bungalow in which they had lived in Motihari, now a dilapidated cow-shed overrun by pigs and stray dogs, was described recently in one Patna newspaper as an "animal farm."

The story that the woman is telling is very close to mine, except that I discovered Orwell when I came to Delhi on a scholarship to finish high school. His essay "Why I Write" was a part of the assigned reading for the same class in which I had earlier read Khushwant Singh. When I read Orwell's essay, I didn't know that this famous writer had been born in Bihar, close to my ancestral village. He was an Englishman far removed from me. If I identified with him it was because in his essay he had described a voice in his head, "a continuous 'story' about myself, a sort of diary existing only in the mind," which was "a mere description of what I was doing and the things I saw." Orwell had written:

> For minutes at a time this kind of thing would be running through my head: "He pushed the door open and entered the room. A yellow beam of sunlight, filtering through the muslin curtains, slanted on to the table, where a match-box, half-open, lay beside the inkpot. With his right hand in his pocket he moved across to the window. Down in the street a tortoiseshell cat was chasing a dead leaf," etc. etc.

It is possible we all do this as children or adolescents and then grow out of the habit, unless you are a writer. In my case, I had become conscious of this activity after I began reading literary texts. Orwell was a part of that early education, and in that voice in my head I first found evidence of my authenticity as a writer. I could be in a Delhi Transport bus in Daryaganj, and a voice running in my head would name the objects I saw being sold on the street, their colors, the look in the eyes of the sellers.

I also then read Orwell's essay "Politics and the English Language"; he wanted to promote writing that was unfussy and modest, never calling attention to itself. He was, of course, giving voice to an ideology, a postwar socialist politics. When I first encountered that language, I wanted to make it my voice. It was also a part of my desire, as a postcolonial, to escape the colonial inheritance that said that our use of English ought to be, as Lord Macaulay had intended it, the language of the clerks. My father wrote his letters to us in a stiff, bureaucratic language. In contrast, Orwell advocated simplicity and concreteness in our sentences. Later, my fondness for the Orwellian diction was challenged in the American graduate programs in critical theory where I found myself producing prose that had the consistency of freshly mixed cement. That phase lasted a few tortured years. In my time since, especially in the writing of *Immigrant, Montana*, I was trying to embrace a voice that was not just loud, exaggerated, sexual but also exuberant. In interviews, I would say that English had been taught to us as a language in which we had to do our homework; to write fiction or imaginative nonfiction was to find a liberation in language. That feeling of freedom is what now seems to make writing most real to me.

Authenticity, or what you call your own or adopt as your own, is to a large extent based on your education. Orwell was a part of my education. So, too, was Naipaul. But that was long ago. There have been other influences. Even during those years of indenture-ship to academic language, I was drawn to the lucidity and playful-ness of Salman Rushdie and Hanif Kureishi. The boldness and invention, not to mention the rage, of Arundhati Roy and Kiran Desai. I was in my twenties when I discovered the mixed-genre ge-nius of John Berger, and his work has never ceased to impress me. He taught me that my authentic voice came not from being an artist or a critic but from bringing those two separate beings to-gether. Today, I see that kind of mixing of voices or selves in other work like Claudia Rankine's *Citizen* and nearly everything that Teju Cole writes.

## 9.

"Authenticity comes from a single faithfulness: that to the ambiguity of experience." (John Berger)

## 10.

A sidenote on authenticity:

For years, I have asked freshmen students in my composition class to read Orwell's essay "A Hanging." The prisoner is "a Hindu, a puny wisp of a man, with a shaven head and vague liquid eyes." We meet the head jailer, Francis, "a fat Dravidian in a white drill suit and gold spectacles" who says things like "All iss satisfactorily prepared. The hangman iss waiting. We shall proceed." This portrayal makes me slightly uneasy, but I don't want to linger. I want everyone's attention focused on a single paragraph that comes later. This particular paragraph contains a description of the prisoner's walk to the gallows: "He walked clumsily with his bound arms, but quite steadily, with that bobbing gait of the Indian who never straightens his knees." Does this description also produce a sense of discomfort in me? It does. But I have nothing enlightening to say about my discomfort, and usually I remain quiet about it in class. What I want my students to grasp is the brilliance of what follows the mention of the prisoner's gait. Orwell writes: "At each step his muscles slid neatly into place, the lock of hair danced up and down, his feet printed themselves on the wet gravel. And once, in spite of the men who gripped him by each shoulder, he stepped aside to avoid the puddle on the path." That closing line is such a marvel of observation that we don't even need the commentary that Orwell offers in the paragraph that follows: "When I saw the prisoner step aside to avoid the puddle, I saw the mystery, the unspeakable wrongness, of cutting a life short when it is in full tide."

To be a writer is to notice and record such moments. These moments that tell us we are alive and that our humanity breathes in us, etc. This is a familiar lesson that I repeat to my students and, equally important, to myself. But then I happened to read the following in James Wood's *How Fiction Works*:

> The avoidance of the puddle would be precisely the kind of superb detail that, say, Tolstoy might flourish; *War and Peace* has an execution scene very close in spirit to Orwell's essay, and it may well be that Orwell basically cribbed the detail from Tolstoy. In *War and Peace*, Pierre witnesses a man being executed by the French, and notices that, just before death, the man adjusts the blindfold at the back of his head, because it is uncomfortably tight.

When the pandemic started last year, I was part of an online group that was reading *War and Peace*. Upon reading the part about Pierre witnessing what Wood describes above, I felt certain that Orwell had borrowed his scene from Tolstoy. Did I feel that I had been cheated? Yes, but only because Orwell's essay is supposed to be a piece of nonfiction. It would have been different if it was fiction. In a novel like Teju Cole's *Open City*, which is one of my favorite novels of the past decade or so, I admire the parts where I hear the echoes of the influence of other writers; not just W. G. Sebald, with whom Cole is often compared, but also, say, the James Joyce of *Dubliners* whose prose about snow falling all over Ireland is transposed into a fine passage by Cole about rain falling over Brussels and "on the preserved cities farther out west, on Ypres and the huddled white crosses dotting Flanders fields, the turbulent channel, the impossibly cold sea to the north, on Denmark, France, and Germany"; or a mad scene involving unruly children and a real, live baby bear in Penelope Fitzgerald's *The Beginning of Spring* transferred to a funeral scene in Lagos and the disruption of a broken vase and the laughter of children; or smuggled into the narrator's reflections in a Manhattan apartment an unattributed riff first delivered on stage by Hamlet at the Globe Theatre. Our writing is always filled with other voices, and authenticity, if that is the word I want here, lies in our exercise of skill and cunning in making those voices our own. My writing goals, likely unreachable, include making the satirical setup of the Hindi classic *Raag Darbari* by Srilal Shukla, or Upamanyu Chatterjee's *English, August,* so much my own that I am able to write an original masterpiece of comedy about the Indian hinterland.

## 11.

In a 1997 interview for *Brick* magazine, Sebald told James Wood the following: "I think that fiction writing, which does not acknowledge the uncertainty of the narrator himself, is a form of imposture and which I find very, very difficult to take. Any form of authorial writing, where the narrator sets himself up as stagehand and director and judge and executor in a text, I find somehow unacceptable. I cannot bear to read books of this kind."

I am of the same view. So, the voice of a narrator struggling with truth, indicating with a pointed finger the joints in the scaffolding, is also mine. I don't know what the term *autofiction* actually means, but reviews of my last novel often used the term. (The review in *The New Yorker* also used the term "non-fiction novel," a description I hadn't heard before and maybe did not even consider possible.) But I believe that a piece of fiction, and even nonfiction, becomes more authentic when it shares with the reader information about how it is put together. I got support for this thinking from David Shields's *Reality Hunger: A Manifesto,* which also promotes the idea of writing as an assemblage. "In collage, writing is stripped of the pretense of originality and appears as a practice of mediation, of selection and contextualization, a practice, almost, of reading." This present piece, in its arrangement and use of quotations and in its attempt to find momentum not from narrative but from the more subtle buildup of thematic resonances, hopes to mimic the lessons of *Reality Hunger.*

## 12.

A month ago, my barber asked me while cutting my hair whether I had watched *The White Tiger* on Netflix. I made a sound, and he said, "It is intense, man, so *real.*" My barber is from Puerto Rico and grew up in New York City. I didn't say anything to him because I didn't want to give him a lecture on authenticity. But if you are interested in my take on *The White Tiger* (the book, not the movie), please read my essay "Bad News" in *Boston Review.**

---

* I should try to watch the movie version too, if only to satisfy my curiosity about how Balram Halwai and his illiterate relatives in a Bihar village, including his old grandmother, sound when they speak English.

**13.**

I was in my twenties and giving a reading in my hometown, Patna. A man in the audience asked me why I wrote in English. What could be gained from writing in this imported tongue? The person who was moderating the session, an admirable cultural activist, chose to answer instead. He said to the audience member, "Excuse me, but even our Constitution is written in English. Which is to say, the Independence we got in 1947 is imported too. Should we throw away our freedom?" I didn't have much to say because this debate was an old and boring one. I am able to write only in English. Often, editors and publishers will have something of mine translated into my native Hindi. Occasionally I'll be reading a piece of my translated prose and I'm pierced by emotion, and I become conscious of goosebumps on my skin.

And this happens not only with my own prose. There is a story I like by the Hindi writer Uday Prakash. It is titled "Tirich." I'm haunted by the names in the story, names of towns, streets, and characters that are rarely encountered in Indian writing in English: Samatpur, Master Nandlal, Pandit Ram Awtar, Sipahi Gajadhar Sharma, Deshbandhu Marg, Sardar Satnam Singh, and, best of all, Satte. The pleasure of coming across, in Hindi, names like Minerva Talkies and National Restaurant! I'm expressing my partiality for this low-rent realism, but it is only a species of nostalgia because, like the members of the Indian cricket team, more and more writers in India these days have their origins in smaller towns and the more far-flung regions of provincial life. And such writers are not likely to remain silent when other, more famous or recognizable writers, from their vantage point in the West, miss important marks of difference. Siddharth Chowdhury, author of such colorful books as *Patna Roughcut,* in an essay called "The Tolstoy of the Biharis" critiques one expatriate Indian writer's portrayal of Delhi's urban spaces: "All the details, the cultural nuance is sandpapered for universal consumption. When he writes about Defense Colony, it might as well be Malka Ganj or Subzi Mandi. The 1990s read like the 1970s."

I feel chastised when I read those words; I have this feeling in my bones that those words must also be true for me. A few years ago, in an essay by Edna O'Brien in *The New Yorker,* I read that James Joyce, working on his great novel *Ulysses* while living in Zurich, would badger his friends for precise information about Dublin—a list of shops, awnings, the steps leading down to 7 Eccles Street. I have followed his example in often asking journalist-friends and family members for information about Patna and other places. If there is a reason why my anxiety about accuracy, which might or might not be the same as authenticity, has been kept in check, it is because of a comment made by Colm Tóibín about Henry James. I liked the comment so much that I cut the section out from the *London Review of Books* and now look at it from time to time. Tóibín assures me that if I get the name of a street wrong, it is still going to be okay if, like James, I plumb the depths of character.

14.

Henry James offered this advice in his lecture on the art of fiction: "Try to be one of those on whom nothing is lost." He wanted writ-

...intellectuals stuck to the question; within four years he would be gone for good.

James did not find his family interesting enough to use them much as models in his fiction; it is possible to find traces of Alice in *The Bostonians* and *The Princess Casamassima*, but of William there is hardly anything. William Dean Howells's unworn diamond became useful when James needed an American character for *The Ambassadors* whose sensuous nature had been stifled by America to be woken – too late – by the glory of Paris. By the time he left America, James's knowledge of its society was deeply limited and seriously etiolated. This lack of deep roots was an enormous help, a great gift, to him in his fiction; it forced him to concentrate on character and style and saved him from writing dull novels about changing social mores or failed dreams in American society.

He based his early Americans on himself and then when he needed...

ers to be curious and notice everything. That is one measure of authenticity. The novelist as one on whom nothing is lost and that often translates into characters on whom nothing is lost. I find this prospect tiresome. Authority stands in for authenticity. (You have shrugged off the desire, or even the need, to find out the number of steps leading down to 7 Eccles Street—and replaced it with your character's worldly omniscience and acuteness of perceptions. Is there a real difference?) My advice to writers is to shrug off authoritative knowledge. You are writing a novel, not an entry for the *Encyclopedia Britannica*. Postcolonial writers, eager to narrate their marginalized histories, produce detailed accounts gleaned from historical and archival research. *Please!* Spare me this Brahmanical impulse! Go back to your temple.

I like characters who, like most of us, are flawed. We struggle with our partial knowledge and our prejudices. We are often wrong. My favorite example here is the comedic jujitsu performed by Zadie Smith in "The Embassy of Cambodia." Her protagonists, Fatou and Andrew, both immigrants from different countries in Africa, are sitting in a Tunisian café in London. Fatou likes having what she calls "deep conversations" with Andrew because he is an educated person with "free, twenty-four-hour access to the Internet." They are discussing the Holocaust. Fatou says, "But more people died in Rwanda. And nobody talks about that! Nobody!" Andrew agrees with her. The writer maintains her silence on the matter; she lets her characters reveal their thoughts. When Fatou shares her view that Africans have suffered the most in history, Andrew wants her to think for a moment. He draws her attention to what happened in Hiroshima. "It was a name Fatou had heard before, but sometimes Andrew's superior knowledge made her nervous. She would find herself struggling to remember even the things she had believed she already knew." This struggle in Fatou's mind makes her remember the relatively recent tragedy of the tsunami. She offers tentatively, "The big wave . . . ," but Andrew with his access to facts will not allow it: "No, man! Big bomb. Biggest bomb in the world, made by the USA, of course. They killed five million people in *one second*. Can you imagine that?"

How wonderful is this!

Andrew is talking back to Henry James: he is revealing the hollowness of a flat, generalizable claim. He is saying, "Mr. James, sir, I'm trying to be one on whom nothing is lost."

## 15.

In the last couple of decades, especially with the coming to prominence of diasporic writers from the subcontinent, the polemic has shifted. The crude charge that is often made against such writers is that these writers living abroad are pandering to the West. A little over two decades ago, Vikram Chandra wrote an essay entitled "The Cult of Authenticity" in *Boston Review* as a riposte to this argument. Chandra's real argument was against a strict kind of moralizing; he was in favor of writing that, to reflect the complexity of lived existence, would be at once local and global. Our lives today, Chandra pointed out, and the lives of the people around us, were irreducibly cosmopolitan. Which is to say, the borders around us weren't impassable. We each carried bits of the other in us. Despite the blistering polemic, much of which I agreed with, a part of me always believed otherwise. And that is why, when a few years later I published my first novel, I titled it *Home Products*. The phrase was borrowed from a quote of Mark Twain's, but the impulse behind it was a simple one. I was reading books by Indian writers in which I would discover very quickly that explanations were being supplied or, worse, matters were being simplified or even distorted for the reader unfamiliar with them. I had begun to think of this latter group of books as products marked for export. As I was writing a home product, I felt emboldened to include in my novel essays on the role of trains in the national imagination, the evolution of love in Bollywood, the status of documentaries. My thinking was that I knew my audience, it was made up of people like myself, and I was opening a door for them. They would enter the door and find themselves in the house in which they had grown up. Their past would become clear to them. And to me.

It is often easy, as in this essay, to slip into memoir. I have a mild distrust of this voice: it is a distrust of the comfort that an easy access to the past offers. It is possible I have on occasion tried to overcorrect this tendency. If you have ever read my essay "Where Is Your White Literature Section?" you will know what I mean. On a friend's suggestion, I walked up to the counter at different bookshops in New York City one fine spring day and asked the salesperson there, "Excuse me, where is your white literature section?" Over and over again, I posed this question to helpful sales staff who—bewildered, patient, clueless, condescending, and, in one case, angry—tried to tell me what to buy. At one bookstore, the nice sales guy said, "*Who* are the great white authors?" Immediately to his right was the seeming answer. Withdrawing a copy of *Freedom* half an inch from its place on the shelf, he gently intoned, "Franzen." He also introduced me to other names: Hemingway, Cormac McCarthy, Philip Roth. In my essay, I talk of how wearying I found the exercise—not just what people said but the pretense I had to maintain throughout, this voice I had adopted as the Sacha Baron Cohen of American letters. I remember thinking to myself that I had dissembled, I had lied, and I would never be allowed to be on *This American Life*. But that unstable margin, where earnestness gives way to exploration and you have found a voice that is unsettling and maybe even disturbing and exhausting, is a place I want to visit again. There is no authentic self if it is not a risky self. Authority is overrated; vulnerability and

cunning are what I want to court. Literature is not an office where
you apply for visas or find guides. I want to will myself to go to that
other, uncertain destination. I'd love to find out how English is spoken there and discover a voice in which to report from that place.

## Reading Suggestions

Svetlana Alexievich, *Voices from Chernobyl*

John Berger, *G.*

John Berger, *A Seventh Man*

John Berger, *The Success and Failure of Picasso*

John Berger, *Ways of Seeing*

Joan Didion, "Why I Write"

Brian Dillon, *Suppose a Sentence*

Vivian Gornick, *The Situation and the Story: The Art
   of Personal Narrative*

David Shields, *Reality Hunger: A Manifesto*

Zadie Smith, *Feel Free*

James Wood, *How Fiction Works*

# On Humor

*Tahmima Anam*

**Let me begin, not with how to be funny, but with the** conditions of possibility that will allow you to write comedy.

How will you give yourself permission to be funny? How will you spread your arms out and make space to tell a story that may not be expected of you?

I will start off with a little story. The story goes like this: it's Halloween, and I've sent my husband and children off to trick or treat because I have another Zoom event to do. Thankfully, this particular platform is not displaying the number of audience members, so I can pretend I'm speaking to thousands of eager readers across the world.

But I'm fading. My Lady Danger lipstick, which I bought for the precise purpose of buoying my spirits, is not working. I can't stand the sight of my face, my tired eyes, that lock of hair that keeps curling in front of my forehead. The doorbell rings. It's definitely a trick-or-treater, taking a chance even though I've switched off all the lights downstairs and roasted the pumpkins prematurely and sadistically. I don't answer, and eventually they give up.

Then the interviewer asks me this:

"You had a great career. The literary world was patting you on the back. Why did you decide to write a totally different kind of book? And looking back, do you think it was a good idea?"

NO I DON'T FUCKING THINK IT WAS A GOOD IDEA

I smile. "Well," I say. "I just wanted to make people laugh."

And then I laugh.

And then, thankfully, it is over.

This brings me to a piece of news, which may or may not be known to you already, which is this: as a writer of color, you are expected to write a certain kind of book. I know this because I wrote three of them, and on my imposter syndrome days (that would be Mondays, Wednesdays, Fridays, Saturdays, and Sundays), I believe this is the only reason anyone ever published me or read any of my novels.

All I ever wanted to do was become a writer. If you're reading this, you know the feeling. That bone-crushing need, coupled with a terror that you may not, in fact, ever be able to string a beautiful, or surprising, or even coherent sentence together. As much as I wanted it, I was afraid that if I tried, I would fail. So I dithered for as long as I could. I did a PhD in order to pretend I was doing something serious with my life, so that my Asian parents could brag to their friends, and so I could earn a 1200-dollar-a-month stipend, live in a derelict pink house in Cambridge, and pay for the occasional burrito at Felipe's without having to get a real job. Plus, there were libraries. Plus, I was really good at bullshitting in class while spending all my time scribbling in the margins of my notebooks.

Being taken seriously has been a major goal for most of my life. I am short, I am brown, I am female, and therefore I have to fight for every cubic centimeter of oxygen I breathe. Sometimes, when I am in a crowded room, people literally don't see me. They just bash into me and say, "Oh sorry, I didn't know anyone was there!" as if to underline how small I really am (as if I didn't know). I actively avoid going to countries where the average person has to comically bend down to speak to me (Nordic countries, I'm looking at you). Being small has always made me want to be big.

This applies to where I come from, too. Growing up, when I told people I was Bangladeshi, they would look at me with pity. "Lots of flooding in your country," they would say, as if they were showing off an advanced degree in reading newspaper headlines. Once, I took a class with a well-known feminist I'd long admired, and when I told her where I was from, she said, "Good for you!" as if I'd just climbed out of the gutter and she could still smell the shit in my hair.

So I armed myself with multiple degrees, learned a lot of big words, and put a "Dr." in front of my name, and this strategy worked, as much as it could work, because I couldn't grow taller or change the fundamental structures of hetero-patriarchy.

But then, the seriousness bore fruit, and something miraculous happened: someone published my first book, a novel set against the backdrop of the Bangladesh War of Independence.

And now, according to this interviewer, I've thrown it all away, because I wanted to make people laugh.

Here is the thing no one tells you when you're a POC writer. You are there to serve a purpose, and that purpose is to tell the world about the place you're from, whether it's a small town in Bangladesh or a council flat in east London. You are the representative of your country and your people.

I don't say this with malice. It's just a fact, and something I wish someone had told me when I was starting out. I wrote three novels set in Bangladesh. No one asked me why I'd written them or whether I thought it was a good idea to write them. No one dangled my literary reputation in front of me and said "Are you sure?"—those novels were the novels I was expected to write, and after I'd written them, I was expected to talk in many forums and in multiple ways about my country, its prospects, its hopes and dreams and failures. I started joking that the Bangladesh government should pay me a stipend for ambassadorial duties.

I was deeply invested in this project. I believed at the time—and I still do—that getting published was a great privilege and that it was my duty to use that privilege to upend some of the stereotypes about Bangladesh that have been lingering in the white imagination for decades. I was single-handedly going to fight against the image people had of my country—an image epitomized by George Harrison's *The Concert for Bangladesh* album cover, which showed a photo of a starving child sitting behind an enormous tin plate, the plate flecked with little grains of rice, as if all the food in the world had already been eaten and this child, gazing tragically to his right, was looking for more.

I would say: we are no longer starving. When religious bigots began attacking writers with machetes, I put on my best "not every Bangladeshi is a fundamentalist" pose and when the Bangladesh government took away the legal age limit for marriage I told everyone about the great strides we've been making in girls' education. I had an answer for everything. All the while I felt it was my mission to fight with that starving child, his pathetic vulnerability a stain on my mission to complicate people's ideas of a place they would probably never see in real life.

Writer, I did my duty. I did it with enthusiasm and joy. But then something shifted inside me. Because throughout that time, that Ambassadorial time, there was another voice inside of me, one that focused less on the state of my country, less about the echoes and reverberations of dark periods of history. The voice was irreverent, funny, scathing, and sharp. The voice liked to curse. It liked to talk about sex and bodies and human foibles. This voice kind of hated the other voice, which it found rather too obedient.

After a decade and three books, this voice would no longer remain on the sidelines. She fought her way onto the page.

I struggled with her. Was she me? Where did she come from? She appeared to have been born sometime in 2013. At the hospital, after I'd had an emergency C-section because I was about to die a Victorian death from pre-eclampsia, my best friend came over with a bag of giant underpants. "You're going to need these," she said, tossing them onto my hospital bed. She came back a few days later, when they still couldn't get my blood pressure down. I was wearing the underpants. "These are poo cupcakes," she said, handing me a box of very dense cakes that had been baked with Things That Make You Poo. We talked about all the terrible things that were happening to my body. We ate poo cupcakes. We laughed.

After I went home with a tiny baby, I spent a lot of late nights texting with my girlfriends. When we talked about those early days of motherhood, the tender, terrifying, vertiginous ups and downs that made us all feel like heroin addicts, I needed a voice that was raw, unmediated, and yes, funny. You really get to know yourself when you have to wake up twenty-three times in the night in order to keep another human alive, all with a stitched-up vulva and breasts like twin torpedoes to which someone has set fire. This is where my funny bone was born; all that terror and joy and sheer relief at being alive needed an outlet.

But the voice had been conceived much earlier. She was the voice of the women in my family. My whole life I've overheard them laughing and whispering and saying shit they would roundly deny in public. My grandmother, who had arthritis and was in debilitating pain for most of her adult life, would always crack jokes about her crumbling bones. She would smile during group photos and exclaim "cheese without teeth!" after she stopped wearing dentures. Her jokes were always self-deprecating and centered on her body as it gave way beneath her.

One summer, when I'd gone home after my third miscarriage, my aunts gathered in our apartment in Dhaka and started mumbling prayers and counting dried beans. I found the ritual humiliating, a public declaration of my inability to have children. But no one took the exercise seriously. One or two of them fell asleep. The rest kept stopping to ask when the snacks would arrive. As the sun set and my mother brought out the samosas and the roast beef, everyone fell upon the food, praising my mother on the juiciness of the meat, then riffing on the theme of juiciness and what made a cook better at getting things to be juicy. In the end, no one said anything about my infertility; they all just laughed and ate and said rude things to each other. That is how it has always been between them, a secret current of belligerence running through the generations.

Yet I was afraid of what would happen if I unleashed that side of me. I was so used to writing—and being read—in a particular way. I didn't know what would happen if I suddenly decided to do something else.

It's not that the world will not accept a funny book from a

brown writer. In fact, there are several types of funny that are wholly accepted, even embraced. Take dark humor. If you write a story about a young boy who falls into a toilet, comes out covered in shit, and then emerges, smiling, to meet Amitabh Bachchan, that is okay. Because the kid is covered in shit, which is kind of funny, but also very, very sad, and it's not ha ha funny, but more like, *damn, that kid is covered in shit* funny. This is okay. You can make white people laugh, but you must make them sad while they are laughing.

There is also the funny that reinforces a stereotype, especially about a woman, especially about a matriarch. I'm talking about the shouty fat woman who barks at you to get married, tells you to become a doctor, then tells you to quit becoming a doctor so you can find a good husband, then tells your daughter to marry a doctor. That woman is a totally okay person to laugh at, because she already exists in everyone's imagination, and you bringing her to life won't disturb anyone's notion of what you are supposed to write.

And finally, there is masculine humor about a fallen politician. If you are a man, you are already winning at life, but if you are a POC man who wants to write darkly about a third-world politician, this is also okay. You can fall into a long-standing tradition of male writers mocking male politicians in that clever, arch, scathing way that will give you serious literary cred. If you are planning such a novel, I salute you. The world is your rose garden.

But lest you think this is just a long list of things you mustn't, or shouldn't, or can't do, let me tell you a few things you can do, once you've given yourself permission to write something unexpected, like a comedy.

First, and most importantly, it is a myth to imagine that writing comedy will take less of your blood and guts than telling a more straightforward story. Comedy won't work if you evade the painful truths of your life. Rather, you've got to bury yourself deep inside them and find a way through to the other side. So, live in the darkness for a while; stay there for as long as it takes. Stare it straight in the eye, and once you've burned yourself up, you will find the funny there. Don't imagine that it exists outside of yourself—that is where stereotypes are born. Both darkness and humor live side by side, in the most hidden, most secret parts of your being.

Adjacent to that thought is this one: the closer the humor is to the pain, the better the humor will be. When you are writing the joke, you won't be laughing, you'll be crying. I learned to tell jokes when my body was at its most vulnerable, in the days after childbirth, when I had no choice but to laugh at how deeply uncomfortable, unfriendly, and unfamiliar my body had suddenly become.

In my latest novel *The Startup Wife*, I wrote a scene between the main character, Asha, and her older sister, Mira, where Mira tells Asha something truly shocking about her post-birth body. Asha is disgusted, she begs her sister to stop, but Mira tells her, "You have to hold [that image] in your big brain along with everything else." And that is the thing about humor: it has to rest alongside the pain, the bodily pain, of being alive. If you tell that truth, you will make people laugh.

When I finished my book, I considered publishing it under a pseudonym. I thought I mustn't spoil my impeccable track record of representing my people. It was tempting to pretend that someone else had written that novel, someone with a clean slate, without the burdens and privileges of an inheritance.

But then I thought, fuck that. This book had come from the exact same place as the others. It had taken just as much digging around in my insides as the others; more, in fact, if you think about where the funny really came from. And it was just as much a part of my history as the geopolitical history that had been the scaffolding of my other novels.

And anyway, I wanted to make people laugh in my own name. So I published that book, and now I get to answer all sorts of delightful questions like that surprise Halloween ambush about whether I have any regrets.

Do I have regrets? Of course I do. I regret the condescension, the way people call my novel "light," the way they subtly remind me that I should've stayed in my lane. But at other—rare—times, I think it's right that I took that space. It's right that I want to be taken seriously and that I want to make people laugh. I want to make them laugh while seeing that everything I say is still as radically political as it ever was. Is that too much to ask? Yes, but only if we accept things the way they are and don't push for change. Writing against the expectations people have of you—writing humor, or genre fiction, or with characters that are unlikable and unworthy of pity—is an act of rebellion, and every act of rebellion creates a little more space for people like us to write things that are not expected of people like us.

As a writer of color, the compulsion to write something that matters, in a world that tells you your story doesn't matter, is always going to be your North Star. These moral urges are impossible to ignore—and they exist for a reason. But I'm here to tell you to take up more space and to write what you want. Don't settle for the same tropes if they don't appeal to you.

If you feel the doubts creeping in (as I do on Mondays, Wednesdays, Fridays, Saturdays, and Sundays), remember that you come from generations of funny. You come from a long line of jokers and laughers. Your people have been laughing through wars and poverty and perilous crossings and bricks thrown in their windows and "Paki!" shouted in their faces. Your people have found laughter throughout the great generational migrations, through revolutions and the changing of rivers and children that have died too soon and parents they have left behind and lands they will never see again. All those ripples of pain and laughter have been passed down to you. They are also your inheritance.

What you do with it is up to you.

## Reading Suggestions

Rokeya Sakhawat Hossain, *Sultana's Dream*
Meera Syal, *Anita and Me*
Mohammed Hanif, *A Case of Exploding Mangoes*
Ali Wong, *Dear Girls*

# On Character

*Tiphanie Yanique*

## THE REAL SELF

**The thing I need us to assume here, the thing I need** us to take for granted, is that as people of color in this historical moment we have hundreds of years of learning the character and characterization of white people, all the while also doing our best to integrate our own sense of strong personal character into a world that denied our integrity at every turn. A world where navigating inside of white patriarchy has been a way to survive. Because of this, we, people of color, have developed a singular awareness of the importance of the interior life. The interior self is the one place where we can be free even if everything outside stands in contradiction to our freedom.

Fiction is an art form charged with revealing the interior life of characters. Fiction writers of color already know, well before any creative writing class teaches it to us, that humans have exterior lives that may be very different from their interior lives, public lives that may be completely disparate to their personal lives. This isn't dysfunction. This segmentation is, rather, a healthy means to survival (as in, I may have to be subservient at work, but when I come home I am a mother, and that means I have a space in which I am sovereign).

This ability, to have an interior life that differs from one's exterior life, is key to the creation of what we sometimes call in craft a round character. Good character development means, in large part, writing each of your people as multiple, contradictory. All real people are thus, of course. Good fiction writers know this about our characters, but not all people know this about themselves. People of color, however, have known this about ourselves since the beginning of Western imperialism. People of color know ourselves to be round long before we understand this as an artistic concept—we live complexly; we live our truths and our fakings, we live in this hyper-seen skin and flesh. We are aware of the making of ourselves in this way; it is a burden, actually. Many who lord power over others have the luxury of self-deception. It is a luxury to be hidden from yourself; it is a luxury to not have to contend with one's own complexities. This is not a luxury of oppressed people.

This is a craft essay that I have written in an attempt to show people of color (who are the main audience of this essay) how to write characters in ways that are not based purely on Western/ white ideals of character development. However, it is important to me that I begin by making plain that I am not revealing any damn thing to you, audience, that you do not already know. You have all along been excellent at developing round characters; indeed, knowing how to create fully fleshed-out characters has been one of the gifts that white supremacy gave you—to see them and know them; to see ourselves and know ourselves; and to be, at times, unknown to *them*.

If you "learn" anything at all from this essay, it will be that when we discover that we are writing one dimensional or otherwise poorly wrought characters, it is either because we have suppressed this complex knowing that we harbor inside of ourselves or because we have "learned" the western idea of character development, which is often narrow, clean, linear, traceable, dichotomous, and lacking in real complexity. This is the character development most often taught in creative writing programs, even ones led by people of color—because it's what they were taught, too. In this way, creative writing programs have led many BIPOC writers away from their own indigenous knowledge, or worse, away from writing altogether. The creative writing workshop is no different than the world.

The gist: since before your own birth this wisdom of character development has been inside of you. The world destroyed you and your people before you in order for you to learn it. Do not let the world take it from you now.

## 1. PSYCHOLOGICAL REALISM

See me, twenty-three. A Black girl from the Caribbean in my first year of an American MFA program in creative writing. I'm in Intro to Fiction. The teacher is a woman, which I think is good for me. But when she hears me introduce myself on the first day she says, "Huh"—as if she knows my name well. That the professors are the ones that rejected or accepted us into that writing program is important here. I knew immediately that this woman had read my file, knew me, but hadn't wanted me. Being unwanted, and having to prove myself, was nothing new for me. My parents had abandoned me as a baby, but with my grandparents' help, I'd managed to craft myself into someone who usually felt worthy of acceptance. I knew, after this woman's "Huh," that another professor had plucked me out of the slush, likely against this woman's wishes. That also was nothing new for me. I'd grown up in a rough neighborhood but had gone to elite institutions, where I was consistently the poor kid. I was used to being underestimated and to surprising people. I was also used to others coming to my support, sometimes unexpectedly (more on this later).

What I hope I am making clear is that the creative writing workshop will destroy you if you are not prepared to stand confidently in your own clarity of thought and talent. And it is also to say that constantly having to prove yourself to people is actually no way to stand in your own clarity of thought and talent. It is emotionally exhausting, for one thing. It can also make it too treacherous for us to experience and communicate our true feelings of vulnerability—a vital and ongoing part of being a fiction writer. We are too busy being justifiably strident. That ethos can show up in our work as didacticism or even diatribe.

In that intro class and in others that year, the author Henry James was regularly held up as a model for us students to follow. Once the professor asked us which other writers we might be able to hold up alongside James. I didn't think it was radical when I answered Gabriel García Márquez. Gabo had already won the Nobel; some critics even thought he was a bit passé. I felt he was important because of his use of magic and myth as a way to communicate ideas about community and nationhood. But the teacher actually turned her whole body to look at me. She said to me, and to the whole class, that García Márquez was not a good example for a writer to follow because, though brilliant, his work was too lacking in logic and therefore could not be used as a model. I could not then articulate why this silenced me, sliced into me. But I can now. Basically, she was suggesting that Gabo wrote with a "natural" genius but that his work was uncrafted, lacking in forethought and intelligence. She looked on him as an idiot savant. Henry James, however, was supposedly more intentional and so therefore worthy of being a model. And the kind of writing James did was called psychological realism.

In the current North American and Western European literary context, much of our understanding of how characters are created comes from a cultural belief in psychology as the primary methodology by which humans come to be fully human. Yes, we have brains at birth, says psychology, but we do not yet have minds. Our childhood experiences and our interpretations of them are the primary factors that shape who we are. Supposedly.

As fiction writers writing in the West or influenced by the West or just pressured creatively by the West because of sales and prizes, we turn to psychological realism as the methodology for creating our characters. Now, don't get me wrong: psychological realism is a useful tool. However, if you have taken many creative writing classes or read American or Western European literature it is likely that you have learned that psychological realism, even if not explicitly called by its name, is the only way, or the *best* way, to craft fictional characters.

Psychological realism is writing a character with awareness of what the character's psychological reality has been. You need to know what happened to your forty-two-year-old character when she was five even though the novel you are writing covers only that year your character turned forty-two. The idea is that inside every forty-two-year-old are the traumas, comforts, and healings of her five-year-old self. In my novel *Monster in the Middle*, my character Fly is mentored by a man who sings a song about a woman named Susanna. This man is the first person—and for a long time the only person—who sees Fly as brave, smart, worthy of responsibility. This fuels Fly's love of music and, later, is one of the reasons he becomes interested in and then falls in love with an actual woman named Susanna.

What is going on emotionally for our characters matters to them as it does to us in real life. But it's not all that matters. One problem is that psychology, along with the craft tool of psychological realism that comes out of it, is a tool that gives primacy to the individual. Psychological realism considers life to be a single, linear journey—and that is often how fiction in this mode is written, with one main character, to whom everyone else is supporting or secondary. *We come into this world alone, and we leave alone.* Many people think this is the truth. Many fiction writers think this is the best way to make a character.

Perhaps you have found this suspect all along.

If you have, this might be because you are pretty sure that you are not alone. That as a person of color, many people (your steadfast parents, your demanding middle school principal, your drug-dealing/-using cousin, your mentally ill neighbor, etc.) have lifted you, taught you self-love, bought you books, praised your talent, made your life possible. Have made *you* possible. You also know that many people (your steadfast parents, your demanding middle school principal, your drug-dealing/-using cousin, your mentally ill neighbor but also social media, visual culture, the news . . .) have crushed you, taught you self-hate and self-doubt, told you reading was a waste of time, encouraged you to "get out there" rather than spend time cultivating your interior life, made your life hard as hell. Again, made you possible. You know you are not you because of your own doing alone. You also suspect that if you had grown up in a different time, near the coast rather than in a desert, or on a mountain rather than in the valley, that who you are would be radically different, straight unrecognizable to whom you have become.

Perhaps there is an essential self, but that essential is cultivated by society. People of color do not have the luxury of going it alone. We know we must roll with our posse, our family—we believe in tribe. We must. It is part of how we have survived.

## 2. SOCIAL REALISM

In my final year as an MFA student I was required to take a class called Fiction Forms. It was a class that many of the professors avoided teaching—what were "fiction forms," anyway? But there was a professor I'd been told to steer clear of who just happened to teach this class regularly. On the first day of Fiction Forms this professor told us, the five or six students who had held out on taking this class before now (hoping perhaps that he might retire), that he had written a handbook on fiction forms. However, he lamented, no one wanted to publish it. He informed us that the reason for this was because he didn't include work by Black people or women as model texts. "But," he clarified, "that is only because I chose the best."

Our class was made up of Black me, a Latinx student, a few white students, and was majority-woman. Clearly this professor had no idea of the social realities of our classroom or didn't care. He was living in some kind of time warp in which the greatest fiction in the English language was not being written by people of color—particularly women of color. He didn't just live in a different America; he lived in a different English. And in doing so he was bereft of the true and great beauty of literatures in English. White supremacy does that to its practitioners. To deny one's social reality is also to deny the full reality of yourself. For example, it was widely rumored that this teacher was an active alcoholic—even other faculty had told me this. In our class, we all assumed that the water bottle he brought to class was actually full of vodka. This man taught his class as if he were an authority over not only writing but everything that was best for us. Yet he seemed unaware that most of us in that class, maybe all of us, considered him utterly incapable of clear discernment. Which is to say, if you want to make fully embodied characters, you need to take their social reality into consideration, even if they don't.

Sociology tells us that our place in society, our family, our intimate relationships—they all impact us. Sociology says that the self is made in relation to others. Our characters are the same.

Social realism is a method by which we can create characters based on their social reality and in doing so create an antidote to the narrow individualism of psychological realism, because social realism considers the current and past communities of the character. Here in social reality, we understand secondary characters as vital—not flat or peripheral but entirely necessary to understanding the so-called main character.

Social realism might even allow us to challenge the whole craft concept of one main character to begin with. An attendance to social realism, for example, allows for the novel-in-stories, in which different members of a family (or of a neighborhood, guests in a hotel, residents in the same apartment complex, a group of friends, etc.) are given fully fleshed-out treatment and are in no way subordinate to one another. I would say that there is no mistake that the novel-in-stories has often been a form of novel writing chosen by women, people of color, and women of color in particular. This novel-in-stories form is one that privileges the social, the community, and argues that a novel may not necessarily (as we have been incessantly told by the Western canon) follow the life of the individual.

The writer crafting in social realism must know not only the major aspects of the main character's life and the major aspects of the characters who impact the main character but also the major aspects of society that impact all the characters.

In my collection of stories, *How to Escape from a Leper Colony*, I write the story of Pinky—a teenager who (spoiler alert) ends up in a car accident. But first we are introduced to a white man, still nursing the pain of youthful heartbreak, who is the proprietor of a coffin shop that Pinky visits. We also are introduced to a priest, from West Africa, who has led a life of emotional restriction that, conversely, has given him the opportunity to travel widely. These people are not Pinky's close associates, but they are members of the island town she grows up in. We learn that Pinky's strict South Asian parents don't want her to leave for college but that her white best friend has a different sense of freedom. The racial and religious dynamics are key to the choices Pinky makes the night of the accident. She's also steered by what it means in the twentieth and twenty-first centuries to fall in love and to be in a group of intoxicated young people. You might also be able to see here that social realism is a tool we can use to value secondary characters. Social realism may even liberate us from the narrow idea of primary characters as the only ones that matter.

If we already write in this mode, it is because we have read many women and/or writers of color. It may also be that we have read American and European literature written before the 1950s. Eric Bennett's book *Workshops of Empire* describes how a national fear of socialism, and the U.S. government's effort to stave off communism, created an entire national literature that turned away from a previously very socially aware body of writing. The American writers who became canonical during and after the Cold War were the ones who learned the idea that good craft is nonsocial, is not for and of the people, is not political. During this period, the social came to be considered both dangerous *and* bad writing.

What did that kind of thinking do to our canon? How did it impact our imaginations?

Before the 1950s, American literature was deeply social, deeply political. It was *The Grapes of Wrath;* it was *The Scarlet Letter.* It was fiction about the impact of society on the character of the characters—and vice versa.

Social realism is, in my opinion, the writing tool that most belongs to the fiction writer. It is the method of character development that most powerfully asserts that *stories matter.* And yet creative writing instructors often steer away from it. That's a damn shame.

Because how could it not matter what is happening in the world politically? Even a first kiss has a political implication. Are your characters kissing for the first time during a global pandemic? Readers who dig what we call historical fiction know this. It's why they dig historical fiction to begin with—because this is a mode of making fiction that doesn't pretend that the politics and culture of the moment don't matter. All fiction really is (should be!) historical. A book is, in its very existence, part of the archive of the time in which it is made. And yet, so much of what we are taught and modeled about fiction is that it should be outside of time, outside of history. How can you make a person outside of history?

Social realism also allows for the impact of the natural and physical environment. This is where the whole concept of the pathetic fallacy comes from. We are impacted by the rain, by the sunshine. How our characters relate to our surroundings affects who they are on the page. We are a different kind of human if we were raised near a sea or on a mountain. Pinky's story, which is called "The International Shop of Coffins," is set on an island. An island, with its contrary mythos as a microcosm and a place of isolation, helps to create a young woman who is very cosmopolitan but also desperate to escape. That the land is surrounded by the sea, that it is beautiful and therefore a tourist destination, that the island had been colonized multiple times and so has unusual driving rules, all impact what Pinky and her friend do that night and what is done to them. This seems obvious, right? But if you have been writing for a while and not deploying social realism, you will be able to look back at your own work and see how many scenes you've written in which characters, for example, are outside, yet the terrain seems irrelevant. Which it *so rarely* is.

Social realism and psychological realism take into account our interior self and our social self, and they can both help us create more rounded characters. Yet we all know that we are not just what happened to us and who and what we are surrounded by. Humans are not only our minds and our societies. It's hard to have a person on the page if that person doesn't have a body.

## 3. BIOLOGICAL REALISM

A poetry class led by Claudia Rankine that I took halfway through my creative writing program clarified for me the importance of the body in literature. We read a poem by a white poet who also taught in the program. In the poem, the speaker refers to the tennis player Serena Williams and says that he can't root for her because she isn't of his tribe. The speaker, we come to understand, is white, and the implication is that he considers whiteness to be the defining factor of his tribe.

We all wondered how the actual poet explained his poem. Did he admit to being racist or was he, maybe, working through ideas of racism in the poem? Professor Rankine invited the poet to our class, where we asked him this very question. His response was that the poem was not racist at all, nor was the speaker of the poem, nor was he, the poet. His evasion clarified, at least to me, that he wanted the poem to be provocative, and he also wanted to be let off the hook for the provocation. But his poem, as writing often does, betrays and reveals him. When I argued that his explanation didn't hold up in the poem, he said: "Well, shoot me already." So I cocked my fingers and shot him with air bullets. Which was only metaphorical but was still, as metaphors can be, satisfying.

The thing the poem was not denying, regardless of whether you agree with my assessment of it or not, is that bodies do matter. In fact, the titillation of the poem depends on us acknowledging the bodies of its subjects—both as raced and as gendered.

Our bodies matter.

And yet, prudish ideas about the physical realm have caused us, in life and fiction, to fetishize the body, which then causes shame, which then means the body is now too much a sight of debasement to be worthy of high art. It's more intellectual, more *literary*, to keep bodies mostly off the page. So we smartish ones leave the body to the bodice-ripping romance novelists—at a cost to the vitality of our own writing.

Again, people of color know the body matters. It's the thing that we are most aware of, it is what the prejudice against us hangs on. We know that our very skin color or nose shape or lip fullness or kink of hair has allowed someone else to legally oppress us. Black people in the Americas know that when we escaped chattel slavery we were claiming our freedom, but we were also claiming our physical bodies back from the master who stole them.

If your body has not been used as an excuse to destroy you, perhaps you can claim that the body doesn't matter. Biological realism, as a method of crafting characters, calls bullshit on the whole concept of a piece of fiction in which race is unmarked because it supposedly "doesn't matter." Because we, people of color, know that race matters. And in fact, we know that white writers telling us that it doesn't matter is a kind of emotional violence based on a disingenuousness that leads to a real, beyond-the-page violence.

This is why I get enraged when a text pretends to not be about race, ignores race, but then suddenly the previously "unraced" character walks into a store and there is an "Asian man" behind the counter. This, as I see it, reveals the fundamentally racist nature of that text: that every character has actually been white and that the author of the text has been convincing us readers that whiteness is universal and therefore need not be marked. And my fellow people of color, whenever someone tells you that something you know to have consequences as deep as death does not matter, you must see this someone as fundamentally lying, as fundamentally dangerous.

Biological realism says that race matters and also that a whole lot of other things matter too: hormones, height, physical ability, perceived attractiveness, age, how a character is clothed and shod, how a character responds to inebriation. In *Monster in the Middle*, Fly is tall and handsome but unable to control his pubescent body. He is good-looking but goofy, emotionally anxious but ambitious. He is Black and a teenager. One chapter-story in the book leans on these physical realities to communicate who Fly is and what options are available to him because of who he is physically: everyone wants him to play basketball, but he can't figure out how to get peers to like him. He is horny all the time but isn't mature enough to manage this—choosing instead to calm his anxiety by getting high and losing himself in fantasy.

This is biological realism. It also clarifies basic shit, like that wearing glasses matters—because a whole plot could turn on a moment when they are fogged because you are wearing a mask during a pandemic.

Your fiction is lifeless without the body.

Often, however, we have made or read fiction where aspects of body are labeled randomly as if they are irrelevant—green eyes, black hair, milky skin. Irrelevant, because why do the character's green eyes matter in this moment of this scene of this story? Or when we see physicality used to quickly and flippantly "flesh out" (a phrase that itself references and honors the physicality of people) a secondary character. Green eyes don't mean anything until you show what they mean. In *Monster in the Middle,* Fly's brown skin and his height are important when he meets the book's other main character, Stela. His physicality reminds her of someone in her past who was focused, driven, and invested in other people—traits that Fly does not actually possess but that nonetheless lead Stela to consider Fly as a romantic option. How he looks misleads her; who among us has avoided this mistake? We must make the physical matter in fiction, as it does in real life.

If you hadn't already, by now you may be realizing that considering all the ways in which real humans are made is not going to make creating fictional characters any easier. It was simple when all you had to think about was whether your character was abused as a child or whether he was loved by his mother. Now I'm telling you that you also have to think about your character from the beginning of time, from all ends of the earth, from foot bottom to head top. You have to think about building a person like God might. Which brings me to my last point.

## 4. MAGICAL REALISM

I understand that I am who I am based on the lore I have been told about my family, the myths of the people I come from, and the faith systems in which I abide. I bring this, too, to my fiction. Strangely, the class in my creative writing program where I learned most how to honor the magic of belief was a nonfiction course. The teacher was a long-form journalist. He never took coincidences for granted. He saw people as more than flesh and blood, but also as spirits connected to the past and the future, and allowed them to be such in his own work, encouraged us to consider the same for our own. We read our work in class and he would ask: what is the reader sup-posed to believe? And he would ask us writers what we believed.

There was a student in the class, not me, who was writing about the incredible horror of her mother being murdered. The teacher encouraged this student, and all of us in class that day, to consider what we believed about mothers and about death. This, he said, im-pacted how the author wrote and how we would read the piece. How does the author understand her mother's spirit or lack thereof? How might the reader understand the finality of death?

Fiction, however, has often steered away from considering be-lief. We are uncomfortable with belief. Belief doesn't seem intelli-gent, and it certainly doesn't seem literary. And yet, to avoid belief is to avoid a deep truth about humanity. Belief in things for which we have no facts to back up has always been part of being human.

Magic, as we may have been led to understand it, is something fake. Magic is something we have been trained to understand as a spectacle and as something that we might find joy in by unveiling its mechanisms and even exposing it for its trickery. The idea then is that magic is not real, that people who believe in magic are fools, and that people who present you with things that science does not yet explain are quacks.

Magical realism is something altogether different. There are no coincidences in magical realism—there is only the understanding or lack of understanding of symbols. Magical realism says that life is teeming with meaning and that belief is an invitation to a more meaningful life for the reader, too. The pleasure for the audience here is not in unveiling but in relishing. Magical realism says that an attentiveness to the unexplainable or the difficult-to-explain is the very thing we need to transform our lives into something profound.

Another way to say this is that magical realism communicates how each of us might be magical, might be the magic.

It is no coincidence that the literature we call magical realism is most often written by writers who are descended from people or parts of the world that have been oppressed by white supremacy—Africa, Asia, the Caribbean, the Middle East, Polynesia, South America, as well as Indigenous and diasporic Jewish cultures. (You, basically.) For many peoples under the weight of generational oppression, belief was often all we had. Facts: It is not possible that a group of Black enslaved people disconnected from education and their own history, taught in their every interaction with white people that they are inferior to those people, can rise up and defeat Napoleon's French empire and gain not only their manumission but make a new nation. Haiti is impossible. And yet, Haiti really exists.

Many Caribbean people will tell you that it was magic of voodoo/vodun that gifted Haiti with a successful revolution. Many historians credit a belief in vodun as a major factor enabling an enslaved people to overthrow a European empire. Magical realism is the literature that can tell this version of the story. Indeed, magical realism is often deployed to tell the big narratives of a culture or a nation—consider *One Hundred Years of Solitude* or *Midnight's Children*. It is the form I used in *Land of Love and Drowning*, my novel that considers how the Danish West Indies becomes the U.S. Virgin Islands. In that novel two girls are orphaned just as their islands are abandoned by their colonial patriarch. The girls are physical embodiments of the islands themselves: both made powerful and abused because of their beauty. As an act of rebellion against the new colonizers, the myths of the islands become manifest in the actual bod-

ies of the novel's main and secondary characters—Kweku, a human,
is also a spider, like Anansi. Youme has a hoofed foot, like the Cow
Foot Woman.

Magical realism is also used to tell stories about major sociopolitical issues—consider *The Mermaid of Black Conch*, a novel about
female subjugation and freedom, or *These Ghosts Are Family*, a novel
about family trauma. In *Land of Love and Drowning*, I use magic to
consider not only the role of family obligations in hurting and holding us back but also the power of unconditional family bonds in
supporting and saving us. Youme's silver pubic hair references an
inherited clairvoyance that connects her to her family's resistance
to colonial and familial patriarchies.

Belief can make you, and your characters, do things that go
against all the logic learned from history, society, and personal experience. Belief can have you resisting the logic of your own body.
In *Land of Love and Drowning*, belief explains why Eeona loves her
abusive father and why Anette lives through a deadly disease. I'm
not saying belief is without its vexations and failings, nor is it always about religion or God. But when your lived experience or
your social reality or even the boundaries of your body make
something impossible, belief can pull you through or pull you
under. How can we makers of humans, fiction writers, ignore this
fundamental part of being human? Conventional ideas about
magic suggest the impossible is just impossible—so why put it in
so-called literary fiction? Magical realism, however, declares that
hope in the not-fully-known is what makes impossible things possible for humans—so you cannot get your characters to their deep-
est profundity without it.

I know many writers who don't "get" magical realism. They

think of magic as gimmicky. I feel embarrassed for these writers. Writing fiction is entirely about wielding magic. Perhaps you can see that fiction writers, as people who deal in symbols, who often link previously unlinked things, are meaning-makers. And so we, as fiction writers, are already believers. We believe that there is a kind of order, a kind of greater mind that is more aware than the humans are—we know this because the fiction writer is the greater mind of the novel or the story. If we believe in nothing else, the writer must believe in herself.

After all, what are you, as a fiction writer, asking of your readers? To answer this, it might be helpful to remember why you first started out loving reading to begin with. Was it because you first saw stories as tricks of language designed to manipulate you into turning the page? Or was the first pleasure in reading and losing yourself, in submitting to the beauty of the words, the mystery of the plot, and the seduction of the characters? Did you suspend your disbelief, did you dive in and, for the time you were reading, become a blessed believer? Perhaps, over time, as you began to think of yourself as a writer, you wanted to discover how the magic worked—how to write a particular type of dialogue, say, or build a scene. Yes, writers, like all magicians or priestesses or prophets, have our tools. But hopefully, you never lost that desire to be swept away; you are learning the tools so that you can sweep your own readers off their feet. After all, aren't you hoping that some stuff you made up can somehow transform a reader's real life?

In that nonfiction class I took, the mother in the essay we discussed was white and the convicted murderers were Black. The essay was, despite its poetic syntax, written with stereotypes of Black sexuality and white purity that made its achievement less than it could have been. The main character, the author herself writing in retrospection, didn't know she held racist ideas about Black desire and white innocence. Because she didn't attend to this belief, her own characters appeared flat—the mother was barely a subject in an essay about her own life and death, the Black men were shadows of toxicity and nothing else, and the whole piece felt contrived. Years later, I read an updated version of this essay where the author did address her own beliefs. In that version, the mother, though still the true victim of the story, is painted with more complexity. On the page, the mother becomes more than her white female body, but also a complex person. Her attackers become men, not just social ideas. And importantly, the daughter, the narrator-writer, becomes a person more freed from her psychological trauma. The essay transcends the "facts" of the murder and presents the child, now woman, the author, as a person truly transformed by her mother's death. The reader can then be transformed, too. Psychology, sociology, and biology, even all of them together, do not do that.

I once dated a man who said that hope was stupid when it came to love. He was in the habit of predicting and expecting the end of his relationships from the very start. Though good-looking and smart, his childhood had led him to think he might be unworthy of love, and so he was morbidly averse to the vulnerability required by love. Hopeful women, like me, wanting to convince him that love was real and could last, had fallen for him his whole life. But all of his relationships ended in straight-up tragedy, as he imploded them with his fear, his lack of belief. This does not work for fiction writers. A fiction writer without hope is, as you may know, a fiction writer unlikely to finish her book. She will self-sabotage. Belief, and the hope it engenders, is a magic spell essential to anyone who has genuine subjectivity in their lives—be it a character on the page or a human in real life.

## 5. OTHER REALISMS

The realisms I have presented to you are the ones I have come to thus far in my forty-odd years as an observer of humans. But you may have made other observations; you may have come to know other realisms. Use those in your own making of humans. Use it all. And, please, as I have done here, share it with the rest of us, so we can all do this good work better. Finally, if it sounds like in asking you to make real humans that I am asking you to do God's work, well, I am. I hope you expect nothing less of yourself.

*Reading Suggestions*

Julia Alvarez, *How the García Girls Lost Their Accents*

Maisy Card, *These Ghosts Are Family*

Louise Erdrich, *The Round House*

Gabriel García Márquez, *Love in the Time of Cholera*, translated by Edith Grossman

Nathaniel Hawthorne, *The Scarlet Letter*

Jamaica Kincaid, *The Autobiography of My Mother*

Toni Morrison, *Jazz*

Monique Roffey, *The Mermaid of Black Conch*

Salman Rushdie, *Midnight's Children*

John Steinbeck, *The Grapes of Wrath*

# On Trauma

*Ingrid Rojas Contreras*

> The political is not topical or thematic. It is not, as its
> strictest definition supposes, something relegated to
> legislative halls, but something enacted wherever power is
> at hand, power being at hand wherever there is a relation,
> including the relation between text and reader.
> —Solmaz Sharif

**When I first arrived in the U.S. and began to study** creative writing, I knew nothing real or deep about the dynamics of power in the mostly white classrooms I frequented, but I could smell them in the air, just as a lamb must smell the possibility of its own slaughter. I was a Colombian immigrant, and I had left my own country in distress. The events of my leaving were something I could barely talk about. They had razed me to brittleness. I staved off panic attacks, marooned to a daily act of managing the intrusive echoes that continued to come years after the fact, and I gave myself to storytelling as to a lifeboat. There were clues of the power at hand in the cursory exchanges I had in the halls of that creative writing department with the white and American-born; in how the natural, discordant follow-up to the unfailing opening question, *Where are you from?* was *Why did you leave?* And in how this, horrifically, branched into an endless array of possibilities:

*But what happened to you, though, if you don't mind me asking?*

*What type of immigrant are you?*

*How are you paying for your expenses?*

*Are you thankful to be here?*

Was this the same as or different from the exacting interrogations I had experienced at the hands of immigration officials to whom I had to make a case for my presence?

In conversation and on the page, not wanting to dwell in an event I was in the process of psychically outliving, I avoided the story of my leaving Colombia. Instead, I wrote experimental fictions full of aftermath scenarios in which no details of the apocalypse that had occurred were disclosed. The story was about navigating the ramifications of ruin. Language fragmented, sense fell apart. My experiments wanted to determine if it was possible to tell a story that was available to me and still deny the white gaze what it most wanted—the graphic details of disaster, the raw implosion as a life came apart.

I wish somebody then would have told me what I know now, that when you withhold a source of narrative tension, you must provide another. Instead, I was given the consensus: these experiments had failed.

One day, at the end of a conference with a professor I trusted, after the feedback had concluded and we were chatting, I shared what I rarely did. I told her about growing up in fear in Colombia, the years of persecution that culminated in a brief kidnapping and forced exile. In that small, windowless room, she sat back in what I can only describe as admiration, and she said, of the worst time in my life, *Wow! You're sitting on a gold mine.*

That trauma is a good thing that happened, that one is lucky to have such material, and that this material is to be exploited for its market value—these notions are common in the writing world; I have heard them countless times. It's callous, but I can understand why some writers arrive at this conclusion.

We are taught that a story is something happening, and in this sense, trauma is the epitome of stakes and risk, a drastic turn of events. Inherently endangering and visceral, trauma is an event through which a person is wounded enough to be changed forever. Their survival is at stake.

Trauma in service of plot is how outsiders often write the experience, but it feels superficial and counterfeit in their hands—a simple page-turning device predicated on suffering. And it can produce a predictable arc: trauma as climax, a savior's rescue as denouement, resolution, and gratitude.

This prescriptive plot—beginning, as it does, with a writer's decidedly political choice of allotting roles to certain characters as troubled and others as liberators—can flatten stories and, if a writer is not careful, produce a facile and binary morality. Canonical novels like *To Kill a Mockingbird* and *Huckleberry Finn*, works of otherwise beautiful craft, and contemporary novels of much lesser, tacked-on craft like *American Dirt* demonstrate how this dynamic can end up collapsing into vehicles of mere *message*. Whether consciously or subconsciously intended, these three books use the trauma of the

Other, of Black and Latine people, to absolve whiteness. By casting a white character as savior, these works hold space for white readers to feel good about a historical or contemporary wrong—in these cases, slavery and its heritage and border violence and its heritage.

Many writers find the literary canon's use of trauma to be so offensive and fatiguing, they will, for many years, for the rest of their lives, avoid writing about their own traumatic experiences.

I encounter this in my own graduate classroom, where I am now the professor. By and large, writers of color who are new to my classroom prefer to avoid writing about their raw experiences, weary of what may ensue. I ask them questions—*Is it that you are not ready to approach the material? Is it that you don't find the story interesting? Is it that you're repulsed by how that kind of story is usually told?* Sometimes the answer to all three is yes.

Readiness can't be rushed, but craft is something we can study even before the point of readiness.

Writing about trauma is a challenge, as, even in the safety of the page, coming close to what has left a psychic injury (and can conjure, at its mention, emotional disturbances and distressing symptoms) is an intense and delicate process.

But for writers of color and queer and disabled writers, this tenuous process is complicated by the commodification of trauma.

To me, the story of my own exile from Colombia and migration to the United States often felt like a politicized territory that didn't quite belong to me, a flag having been planted into it, long before I was born, by a people to whom I was historically illegible, unless I could be understood by my strife.

I was in graduate school by the time the desire to write about this experience took on a high frequency I could not ignore. It gave me pause. Was the determination to write about it born of me, or was it born from the gaze latent in the environment I moved in, which continually asked this story of me? Was I responding to seeing which books populated the bestseller lists and noticing how they told stories of migration by repurposing trauma with the feelings and education of white people in mind?

This was a time when we all suspected but didn't know to be true that the publishing industry skewed white. Now we know it also skews straight and abled. A 2019 Lee and Low Books survey on the publishing industry in the United States—accounting for agents, reviewers, editors, interns, and everyone in between— found the workforce to be 76 percent white, 74 percent cisgender and female, 81 percent straight, and 89 percent non-disabled. The classroom, too, lacks diversity. A 2016 survey done by the Association of Writers and Writing Programs found instructors to be 72 percent white and tenured professors 81 percent white.

What did it mean that the story I wanted to write was also the story that was most often demanded of me?

As I wandered into the discomfort of the question, piece by piece, I found my way.

The story I wanted to tell—that is, Colombia in the '90s with the attendant terrors of that time: Pablo Escobar and car bombs, guerrillas and paramilitaries—was, to my people, overrepresented. Colombians in my life were impatient, concerned that I was reinscribing a stereotype. *Pablo Escobar again? We've heard that story so many times.* Had we? As I sat with their protestations, I realized I disagreed.

Versions in which Pablo Escobar was described with glee and admiration had been written ad nauseam. The most visible version of this story, the Netflix series *Narcos*, was still on its way, but we had seen iterations of the same framework in lesser-known books and films for many decades. In these iterations, the point of view was Pablo Escobar's or as close to his as possible. This particular choice, and the requirement that the story be accessible, attractive, and interesting to a (white) reader or viewer, tended to result in an idolization of Pablo Escobar's intelligence. It glossed over the psychotic killings and brutal gender violence endemic to the Medellín Cartel and realigned his morals with Robin Hood's (even though he had talked about charity as a psychotic person might, calling it a campaign to trick people into rooting for him so that he could become invulnerable). What had been traumatic for many of us—the violence we had witnessed and lived through—came back to us stylized, sexualized, devoid of consequence, and stripped of emotion.

But mine was a calling to correct a narrative that sided with aggressors and to name what had happened, not from the outside but from within—inside the minds of two young girls in a quiet house. I wanted to portray how violence changed a person, slowly and over time; how it remodeled language; and how it engendered its own altered time and reality. I wanted Escobar to be ever-present like the weather, important and large and also, somehow, insignificant; and I wanted, most of all, to tell a story that centered victims, young girls at that, and delve into what girlhood meant amid the slow-boiling erosion that is living in fear. It was not the same story at all.

I saw a stark difference between working in story territory that had been overtaken by outsiders and enacting the same harms done by them. When it came to the risk of self-exploitation, the story of trauma in itself wasn't the danger. The same material can feel gratuitous and exploitative, after all, or human and powerful, depending on who's narrating it and how, and this is craft, and this is lived experience. It's all in the telling.

Yet it isn't a simple matter that can be solved with the choice of point of view. In the case of *American Dirt,* the novel's close third-person point of view ranges between a mother and son who are forced to cross the border, fleeing drug cartel violence, riding atop a freight train with other migrants who are vying to get north and seek asylum. It's presented to the reader from the victim's side, but the gaze is still white, and it fails spectacularly to understand the experience. For much of the book, the source of narrative tension comes from migrants falling into the rails of the train, the gore of which is described in gloating, graphic detail. Far from carrying the authentic pauses and silences and woundedness inherent to going through a traumatic event or holding a hushed reverence for lives lost, this point of view relishes in the violence, is not at all concerned with retraumatizing others, and is banking on the transmutation of trauma as thriller.

Had I not lived my own story, had I not come to know the punctuation of trauma, maybe I would have felt less sure about what I wanted to write. But I had grown up through violence, escape, and migration, and I had dealt with the long echoes of such a coming of age.

The Colombians in my life were not the only ones to offer words of discouragement. Marginalized writers with whom I had previously found allyship advised me to reconsider as I would be adding to an already vast literary catalog of people of color suffering.

What I knew is that no power dynamic should prevent me from

telling my own story, and asking each other to produce work in one tonality also refuses our full humanity. Instead, I heard this concern and knew it meant that if there was tragedy in my story, there should be many dimensions—it should also be full of laughter at inappropriate times, wrong decisions, and an attraction to death when death is on the table, which is what happens in desperate times. I looked to the work of Luis Alberto Urrea, Samuel Beckett, and Franz Kafka, whose journeys into darkness also possessed a feeling of laughing in the dark.

South Americans were weary of stories like mine too, tales about families escaping and finding refuge in "getting saved by" the U.S., but I knew I wasn't in danger of producing that story. What I had lived through was not a simple moral binary, and the characters in my novel, which would eventually be published under the title *Fruit of the Drunken Tree*, would escape violence, but their problems would not cease to exist, magically, as they crossed the border, since they hadn't for me. Instead, the solution of finding refuge in another country would engender its own complications. The initial relief my characters felt would not lead to gratitude but to an irrevocable estrangement from the self and an unnerving and unmoored relationship to home, territory, and the past and the present. They would find refuge, and in the quiet of that refuge, they would understand they hadn't emotionally left the situation they had escaped, and they would have to deal with what it meant to be a racial minority in the U.S.

Trauma would not be a singular and convenient climactic event but a continuously unfolding, glacial distress that altered my characters' language, messed with their sense of time, and made them unrecognizable to themselves and each other.

So I knew, even before starting, where and how I would diverge from the way in which the story was usually told. I had reservations about whether it would save me from self-objectification, but I tried to stay with the certainty that all I had to do was be faithful to my own experience, while allowing myself the freedom to invent. The careful study of exploitative texts had shown me what to avoid. It had given me a clarity about angle and arc, about which bends of narrative led to exploitation and why. Without this, I don't know if I would have arrived at any such clarity.

By and large, most marginalized writers must work in an environment where they collaborate, collide with, and push against a literary industry that is white, straight, and abled. They must consider—be it in the classroom or the publishing process—what happens to their story under the gaze of a people that is used to being the central audience of most books they open.

A marginalized writer's task is dual: telling the story they want to tell and resisting editorial feedback that wants to turn their story into an identity-experience safari, wherever that isn't the artistic intention or the point.

Writers of trauma must additionally guard their own story from the copious tropes that can make the material exploitative.

A familiarity with and a study of exactly why and how trauma feels exploitative on the page is necessary. While reading, a writer should ask: What audience is usually centered, and how and where does this make the literature collapse into *message* or a binary morality? What literary mechanisms are at work that dehumanize the experience? What are common story arcs and what politics do they support? What tropes are part of the true mechanics of an experience and should be incorporated, and what tropes should be resisted? A writer may also choose to write into tropes when parody is the aim.

There was a trope in my novel that I chose to play into, but parody wasn't my aim. It was simply the most authentic narrative choice I could make. I placed the kidnapping at the climax, knowing that it was the moment that changed everything for everyone. However, I resisted feedback that would lead to objectification. I refused to portray the kidnapping in full, as I was centering a Colombian audience for whom such a scene would be retraumatizing. Instead, the kidnapping is something that happens offstage, and when the story is shared, long after the fact, it is told haltingly and in pieces, which is also what I know about how trauma is told.

There are also questions of imagination and invention, and answering these involves tapping into the writer's own experiences. The story choices made when one has lived through trauma and is living *with* trauma—from the handling of time, dialogue, and prose to structure—are different from the ones employed when trauma is used as a simple climactic device. What are the compositional phrasings during a panic attack? How does time bend under the throes of dissociation? How is dialogue clipped during a traumatic episode? Each writer will have their own stylistic interpretation.

Novels such as *On Earth We're Briefly Gorgeous* by Ocean Vuong and *Beloved* by Toni Morrison and the short story collection *This Is Paradise* by Kristiana Kahakauwila deal with trauma in politically and trauma-informed ways. Vuong chooses to withhold the climax of trauma and uses a structure that interprets post-traumatic narrative as a site of wreckage. Morrison chooses to embody trauma in a materialized ghost in the most gorgeously haunting work of fiction I've ever read. And over and over again, in *This Is Paradise*, Kahakauwila expands the dire places of the heart to the ingrained harm of the politics of territory and tourism at work in Hawai'i.

The decision of writing or not writing about trauma should be made from personal preferences and stylistic choices. Stories can be told in trauma-informed ways—and when looking for how to do this, self-observation will be the sure-most guidance.

What are your own intuitive silences around what you have lived through? Which details are withheld and from whom? Which details are shared freely? This patterning is a structure in itself. If followed, this path will lead to a truer way of telling.

In western interpretations, craft is limited to the elements that govern a story. This limitation divides experience from invention and the writer from the page, as if craft were a buttoned-up thing that happened in a lab. My interpretation of craft includes the writer too and, when it comes to writers writing trauma, how words may cause havoc inside a writer and how a writer may safeguard themselves during the creation of their work.

There are myriad symptoms and complications with trauma. Traumatic experiences are singular, and the body handles them uniquely as well. Insomnia, depression, sexual overactivity and inactivity, nightmares, anxiety, flashbacks, guilt, and memory lapses are all the body's way of responding in the best way it can to care for itself through distress.

But I am now bumping into the limits of my own process and experience and what it has meant to my writing practice. Being as limited as I am, I will offer what it's been like for me, with an invitation to see where this strays from your own experience and where you might adapt it to your own needs.

Trauma is a life-changing event, and to choose to write about it involves a lot of care. A writer must be at a place in their life where the readiness to tell is there. But the desire to tell is not enough.

I have tried to write stories too early and caused myself to spiral by coming into contact with material that still had too powerful a hold on me.

Writing always requires higher powers of observation, but I find this to be essential when writing trauma.

When I am writing other material, I aim to get to a place of concentration where I am almost absent from the process, where my body is left behind and I am operating at the borderlands between the conscious and the unconscious.

But when writing trauma, I find it safer to remain embodied, as it is not always perceptible to me that I have begun to be overwhelmed and am beginning to ride an upward ascent that will lead, in a few hours, to anxiety and a panic attack.

Professional help has been for me indispensable, but I know that therapeutic care can be inaccessible to many for a variety of reasons. Through close study and professional guidance, I have learned to recognize my body's particular early distress signals: faintness, dizziness, a sense of being far away, then estrangement.

I have also stubbornly pushed past these signals to find at their other end precarity, dissolution, and mental and emotional breakdown.

There is always a danger of going too far, and you might, as you learn your own edges.

When writing trauma, the two objectives I flit back and forth between are: how not to unravel and how to unravel safely.

One of the functions of writing a story is becoming entranced in the time and place of the story. When this place is from real trauma, it can be triggering, and it can make you believe that you are reliving that time. So to keep myself from traveling fully to that place, I place an uncomfortable rock in my chair and sit on top of it. The jagged edges of it are a constant reminder that I am in my room, writing, that it's been years, and that I am reclaiming what happened to me by telling it again, but differently, making space for the narrative I most need.

Sometimes, even with this safeguard, I become unwell. If I get to a point of dizziness, I stop and shift my focus to care. But even when done safely, the emotional register left behind by approaching trauma will have to be dealt with. Self-soothing, distraction, or doing nothing and feeling what's been unearthed are the options available to me.

The first two are the easiest.

I play with my kitten. I make tea and open the window. I look out of my apartment in San Francisco and appreciate how far I have come. I stretch in the sun or draw a hot bath and go through what my life is now—my circle of friends and family, the love I experience, the responsibilities I have to my students, the fact that I get to make a living out of thinking about and writing stories.

If I want to distract myself, I may go for a strenuous run. I may dance, call my mother. I engage with things that adjust the immense emotion of what I am feeling. I put up my hammock and watch live video feeds of space and think about how I am on the earth watching the earth from space. I sign up to do volunteer work.

If nothing is working, then I make peace with the fact that I will have to sit with the emotional distress. I lie on my couch under a weighted blanket gifted to me by a dear friend, and I feel and listen. This is not easy work. Often, I am in such pain, I am crying. But by making a practice of trying to listen, I can say that over time, it has gotten easier, and I have gotten better at tolerating it.

For many years through the drafting process of my novel, I was confused about my inclination to write something that was so delicate and potentially harmful. Now that the novel has been published and I'm on the other side, I know that the end result is that in retelling the story, in listening to what the experience itself had to say, I can name through my characters how it has altered my life.

Literature is the place we can go to interact with the ineffable. When the place is rooted in trauma, the ineffable is powerful and requires care and attention. Whatever you do, take care. You need and deserve it.

## Reading Suggestions

Matthew Salesses, *Craft in the Real World: Rethinking Fiction*
   *Writing and Workshopping*
Toni Morrison, *Playing in the Dark*
Melissa Febos, *Body Work: The Radical Power of*
   *Personal Narrative*
Ocean Vuong, *On Earth We're Briefly Gorgeous*
Toni Morrison, *Beloved*
Kristiana Kahakauwila, *This Is Paradise*

# On Translation

*Xiaolu Guo*

**One day, in the midst of working on my first novel in** English, I was overwhelmed by a wave of frustration with my adopted language. With some fury, I knocked this out on the page and decided not to translate it:

我说我爱你，你说你爱自由。

为什么自由比爱更重要。没有爱，自由是赤裸裸的一片世界。

为什么爱情不能是自由的？

A few years later, when the novel was published, the Chinese text remained exactly as it was, though the rest of the book had been revised hundreds of times.

I used to write and think in Chinese ideograms. Then, at the age of thirty, I switched to writing in English. But when I write in English, I don't quite think in English. I have to self-translate. Self-translation is not like translation as we might ordinarily know it. It's more dif-

ficult and involves the writer's whole, lived experience. The process
of self-translation and linguistic translation is like crossing a wild
river from one bank to the other. To get across, you have to deal
with treacherous weeds and hidden rocks and whirlpools of culture
and concept. And the other bank is not always in view. But you
swim on.

For a writer coming from an idiographic and pictorial writing
system, this transition to an alphabetic system is complicated.
Of the many differences between the two systems, the first and
foremost is visual. To give a concrete example, in Chinese, a tree is
木 (pronounced *mu*). If you put two trees together, it becomes
a grove—林 (*lin*). And if you put three trees together, it makes a
forest—森 (*sun*). Perhaps because of its iconographic nature, Chinese writing is more condensed—each symbol holds more meaning than a word. It's also nonspecific about time and action. If one
reads a Tang poem and its English translation alongside, one quickly
gets a sense of the difficulty of the translator's task. All the basic
structures such as subject, action, and specific time have to be pro-
jected by the translator onto the ideograms. There's a beautiful simplicity in one tree being 木, two being a wood, three a forest. But
such an imagistic mode of conveying meaning leaves the European
translator floundering.

But I am not here to talk about untranslatability. On the contrary, I want to talk about the possibilities of translation. I especially
want to discuss the layers of self-translation migrant writers have to
undertake when they write in a new language and culture.

When I am beginning a novel, there are two fundamental things
I need to establish. One is horizontal, the other vertical. The horizontal is the landscape. The vertical is the social space. These are

the dimensions that allow my imagination to enter my novel and people it with characters. I know for certain that when I write in Chinese, landscape comes first. I must know if I am writing about a village or a city and whether it is an agricultural village made up of cultivated land and animals or a car-choked city full of workers and the newly rich. Then the architectural elements come in—whether it is an apartment in a tall, modern building or a traditional court-yard. Characters are tied to their living spaces, and their development is tied to the changes in that space. So I construct everything around these two horizontal and vertical elements. The characters are depicted through their particular forms of language, be it their dialect or a common form of speech—in China, almost every region has its own dialect, and Mandarin is an official language that is mostly spoken in the northern part of the country.

These ways of constructing a story had hardly altered when I began to write in English after moving to Britain. But somehow, in English, I could not just depict a Chinese landscape or its living history as I had done in Chinese. This was not a mere matter of linguistic translation (which is hard enough) but of a deeper matter concerning the translation of the writer's self. By "self" I mean that reservoir of memories and experiences that cannot be separated from cultural and political conditioning.

As a writer who has migrated from a culture far from the European tradition, what I must confront with the alphabetic language (in my case the English language) is the chasm of cultural differences mixed up with mutual ignorance of one another's history. I cannot just wait to be understood. It's up to me as the writer to build a bridge spanning this abyss. Maybe one day Westerners will wake up and realize the importance of Asian culture, open the first page of *Dream of the Red Chamber* or *The Tale of Genji*. But until that happens, I must self-translate. I must convey my voice, culturally and politically, in a second tongue in order to influence my new readership. The way to do this is through the creation of a hybrid language. To self-translate, one has to hybridize language. Chinese concepts that naturally live in the world of ideograms must be re-cast in English idioms and syntax.

I am the complex product of Confucianism, Buddhism, and Communism mixed up in a country newly opened after centuries of self-isolation. Ancient Chinese poetry as well as modern authors such as Lu Xun and Eileen Chang are my foundations. I was also attracted to foreign works in Chinese translation: the Japanese authors Kawabata and Mishima, the Indian author Tagore, and Russian authors, especially Dostoevsky and Chekhov. The poetic and epic traditions in those works were the backbone of my literary imagination. But as I grew into my twenties, I turned to the West. Twentieth-century authors such as Duras, Sartre, Beckett, and Calvino, as well as the Beat Generation poets, began to play important roles in my literary experience.

But nothing is more significant than one's own early physical and sensuous experiences. My hometown, Wenling, is a semitropical mountain region in Zhejiang Province. I grew up there after some years of living in a fishing village. The town and I both underwent huge changes. I turned from a skinny, snot-nosed, lonely girl into an adolescent hungry for escape, while my town grew from a small agricultural settlement—*xian*—into a bustling city—*shi*—of 1.4 million inhabitants. Today my hometown is full of brand-new, cheaply constructed skyscrapers that cast shadows on peasants trudging along motorways with their root vegetables stuffed in shoulder bags. Before the 1990s, the area was an agricultural valley with tea bushes and bamboo forests on the horizon. There was no tunnel going through the Yandang Mountains and the Wuyi Hills. The highways were only built in the 1990s. We never left the town, and we walked everywhere within it.

When I was still in primary school, in the 1970s, I would walk from our house under a hill bristling with bamboo, eventually arriving at the school, which was located at the foot of a mountain—*Hushan*, the Tiger Mountain. Often I was late for class because on the way I would lose myself in the brilliant bright blooms of rapeseed fields. The yellow flowers stretched beyond the reach of vision. My feet would get stuck in the mud where buffalos soaked themselves in muddy streams. Wiping my wet shoes on the grass, I'd then turn onto a dirt road and pass a factory where plastic goods were produced. The little creek in front of the factory was tinged with purple, red, and blue—the chemical materials used to color the plastic wares. As a child, ignorant of its poisonous nature, I found the colorful water a wondrous phenomenon, and I would soak my hands in it. I remember collecting bunches of plastic strings from the factory's dumping ground to take to school. During my excruciating math class, I made plastic shrimps and bracelets with them. In the break, we girls would compare our handicraft. Our palms and fingers would be inked in red and blue. But we didn't know those words then—*cancer, pollution.* Those terms entered our minds only in the 1990s.

I remember during our school lunch hours, students could either return home or eat in the canteen. Sometimes I'd grab a few pork buns from the canteen and climb up Tiger Mountain. There it was easy to sense that, indeed, a mu is a tree, two mu is a wood, and three is a forest. Everywhere I went as a young girl, there were large-leafed semitropical trees. Wherever there were no trees, there were crops in fields. Sweet potatoes, rice, tea, wheat, mandarins, and watermelons. Farmers and craftsmen lived next to the fields and mountains, working, sweating, swearing, and struggling.

How much have that life and that landscape shaped my sense of being in the world? And how to render that life in English in a narrative form? It seems essential that I deliver that past and that sensibility in my writing if I am to communicate my view on my current life, a Western and urban one, caught between cultures and languages. That process is to me a self-translation, as a writer and as an immigrant from a faraway place. I have decided to make a home in the West and to write in English. So I have had to search for a writing style that is not typical British English or American English but a self-made Anglophone prose that expresses a sensibility, and narrates a history, unique to the storyteller. I am aware that the voice in my Western books has always been changing, always evolving. I feel that all my writing life has been a voyage of discovery, searching for that voice, a voice that can be grasped and also appreciated by my readers. My readers now, not being Chinese, may not fully comprehend my writings. But whether or not these readers are politically engaged or apolitical, I have a minor responsibility to remind them of the multiple identities of my characters. All of us have multiple identities, but we don't always realize or acknowledge it. This multiplicity means that one language is not enough to fully understand the world, just as knowing only one kind of climate is insufficient to understand nature. If we live only in one language, we miss something about the world.

When I was writing *A Lover's Discourse,* my most recent novel in English, the same elements—landscape and architectural living space—were decided before the story. Perhaps "decided" is not the right word. It is more that they chose me. The Regent's Canal area in northeast London is the novel's geographical setting, as is the ever-expanding immigrant scene. The winding, narrow English streets and the wet parks are the spaces my characters move about in. Along with those choices, I could not help but absorb the political atmosphere after the Brexit referendum. That naturally led to me putting another European country (Germany in this case) as a place of possible refuge for my two non-British Londoners. Would they move to Europe or return to Asia? Both were transplants: Where was their home? What could their relationship to Europe or Asia be? When I thought about these themes, I could only write in a comparative mode. I kept comparing the sky and the water of England to the sky and the water in China. I kept comparing daily life in the uncertain political environment of Britain to daily life in China. I thought of the difference between a democratic society such as Britain and an autocratic one such as China. I thought of how the West's ideology of the pursuit of happiness compares with the East's pursuit of harmony. I translated my feelings into sentences and dialogue, putting them into the characters' mouths and minds. My English sentences were tinted with a particular East Asian past: Confucian tradition and nostalgic romanticism fused with the sloganistic communist language. Although that past was not entirely present in my novel, it built the tone of the book, its voice. It's in the voice of a female author from mainland China who has tried to adopt Western culture by living in it and conversing with it. That's also how I wrote my previous novels *I Am China* and *A Concise Chinese-English Dictionary for Lovers*.

But to self-translate is to study what surrounds me in my present life and how it relates to my past experiences. The past is always the subtext and a strong ongoing memory. Since I have been living in this part of Europe, I am cut off from an agricultural life or a collective way of living. Still, I search for them in my foreign existence. Every day, my walks take me to the paths where English nettles and wild elderflowers grow. My wanderings frequently lead me along the canal's rust-colored waters, either toward the west, to Islington and Angel, or toward the east, to the Olympic Park and the Lee River. I can't remember at which point I began to see urban beauty in these decaying industrial remnants. It makes me think of the former glories of Britain now forever lost. For a Chinese, this aesthetic is alien, but I have managed to grow into it. Like England's cloudy skies, like baked beans on a breakfast plate, like pale faces and muddied boots. These facets of life have been in my routine since I arrived. So the characters in my Western stories live with these landscape elements, along with European and American politics. But where does China fit in? For me China lies everywhere and is beneath everything. China formed the mind's eye that I carry with me, through which I view everything, coloring the world with shades and hues. I must bring it out through my writing. This is the self to be translated.

* * *

I come from a tradition of artisans and craftsmen. My father was a fisherman-turned-painter, self-taught, like most artisans of his generation. People from his generation were skilled with their hands. They were calligraphers, carpenters, tailors, trumpet makers, silk weavers, and porcelain producers, and they taught their children their skills by working together with them. I wanted to write about that tradition, but in a reflective way. I wanted to write about it in the context of a global environment. That's how I came to write about the female protagonist in *A Lover's Discourse* visiting an artisan village. I recalled my experiences of visiting Dafen village near Hong Kong, which specializes in copying classical paintings. The landscape there is tropical. In the narrow streets, husbands copy Renaissance paintings from Da Vinci or Botticelli; wives work on modern or postmodern works by Monet or Chagall. Their children play in the background while grandmothers chop vegetables and meat. When I was staying in the village and interviewing the painters I took this all in with quiet amazement. It was a flow of life without the need to define itself. The harshness of economic pressure in these people's lives was transmuted into an almost meditative lifestyle. You could call this a kind of stoicism, or self-effacement. And for me it is the kind of life I want to portray in my "Western" novels, highlighting the contrast with lives in the West. This prompts me to ask many questions. How does that kind of working life produce a global consumer culture? And why does the West hold such a prejudice against the Chinese way of thinking and working? Why don't they realize that the Chinese labor market is part of a postcolonial legacy, the monstrous product of Western power? By touching on these questions in my writing, I return to my early life and mine it for rich details.

Still, I feel that I am swimming across the vast river, in mid-stream. My body is tangled in weeds, caught up in passing branches. My arms are heavy. I am trapped, and I try not to drown. I struggle to find my way out toward the other side of the river.

All translation is simulation. Simulation is the attempt to reproduce the effects of something in another medium. But one cannot reproduce exactly the same expression in another culture or language. There is no such thing as a perfect translation or even a right translation. For example, Chinese speech and literary works tend to use lots of metaphors, perhaps partly because of its ancient history and poetic tradition. We say "flowing water does not rot" (流水不腐), meaning a healthy life is one that keeps moving and welcomes change. We say "when the tree falls, the monkeys will be scattered" (树倒猴散) to speak of the fragility of fortune. We say "throw a brick to get a jade" (抛砖引玉), meaning to toss an idea around in order to attract real wisdom. We say "move a tree it will die, move a man he will live" (树挪死人挪活) to mean that human life is about doing things actively. But if one translates these metaphors directly into English without reinventing them, they sound false, especially to European ears. The word *translate* betrays itself. The word comes from the Latin verb *transferre,* meaning "to carry across." A good translation is never really a translation. It is a creative reproduction. A translator who undertakes the task of translating Homer's *Odyssey* attempts to capture the emotional effect of people from that time. But how do you capture that? It does not happen if the translator translates word by word in a technical way. It is necessary to capture the poetic force in a given language despite the historical gap. The English playwright George Chapman managed this feat. His translation inspired Keats to write a poem entitled "On First Looking into Chapman's Homer":

> Oft of one wide expanse had I been told
> That deep-brow'd Homer ruled as his demesne;
> Yet did I never breathe its pure serene
> Till I heard Chapman speak out loud and bold:
> Then felt I like some watcher of the skies
> When a new planet swims into its ken.

Keats was amazed by Chapman's alchemy, his transmutation of the unknown ancient world into a living English.

Another example is the ancient Chinese text *I-Ching* (sometimes translated as *Book of Changes*), perhaps the most difficult Chinese book to translate. It is difficult not because it is written in *guwen*— the ancient and almost dead Chinese script—but because its cosmological and philosophical content is hard to interpret. Western translators have to make conjectures based on research and through comparison of different sources. I cannot believe that any foreign edition of *I-Ching* could work without a certain degree of reinvention and even free interpretation in the target language. I salute those who have undertaken such a painful task. Without them, we would still be living in the dark. But the significance of one particular type of literature is down to geopolitical influences. The Bible achieved its global influence by appearing in every major language (and through the machineries of colonialism), whereas *I-Ching* has not and will never have a similar effect. The geopolitical map is really the core of things, and we writers, especially the writers from the non-Western world, are engaged in an almost Sisyphean task: the rock of our work often slides back down the hill, but now and then we can get the rock to stay on the top of the hill.

The writing of dialogue is another source of difference between nonwhite and mainstream western literature. In my opinion, there is more oral tradition and more folk references in the dialogue of non-European authors. For example, in V. S. Naipaul's *A House for Mr. Biswas*, the dialogue seems to render effortlessly an oral history of where the author came from. Naipaul's dialogue is rich in detail and has a fable-like quality. It often reads as unreal and symbolic, like a Buddhist text or a Hindu myth. Look at any page of *A House for Mr. Biswas*. When Mr. Biswas's son is born, the midwife says: "Whatever you do, this boy will eat up his own mother and father." Then the village pundit responds: "The only thing I can advise is to keep him away from trees and water." And he continues: "Keep him away from rivers and ponds. And of course the sea. And another thing . . . he will have an unlucky sneeze . . . much of the evil this boy will undoubtedly bring will be mitigated if his father is forbidden to see him for twenty-one days."

For a reader like me, this kind of speech feels familiar, like a homecoming, even. I feel as though I am reading a Chinese novel set in a swampy southern village inhabited by gossiping ladies and buffeted by stormy typhoons. This vivid oral tradition is something very close to the narrative tradition in which I built myself as a writer. The same goes for *The Palm-Wine Drinkard* by Nigerian author Amos Tutuola. I connect instantly with its wonderful sense of folk speech, which is not neat or controlled but improvised, ever-shifting, and full of repetitions. I love its wild but simple and folksy qualities, and I never felt it was alienating or strange. *The Palm-Wine Drinkard* is a hybrid transcript of pidgin English and local dialect. A typical paragraph from the novel shows its fantastical vision of brutal realities:

> We met about 400 dead babies on that road who were singing the song of mourning and marching to Deads' Town at about two o'clock in the mid-night and marching toward the town like soldiers, but these dead babies did not branch into the bush as the adult-deads were doing if they met us, all of them held sticks in their hands. But when we saw that these dead babies did not care to branch for us then we stopped at the side for them to pass peacefully, but instead of that, they started to beat us with the sticks in their hands, then we began to run away inside the bush from these babies, although we did not care about any risk of that bush which might happen to us at night, because these dead babies were the most fearful creatures for us. But as we were running inside the bush very far off that road, they were still chasing us until we met a very huge man who had hung a very large bag on his shoulder. . . .

Despite the current debate on the self-colonization of African writers in the discussion of postcolonialism, for me it is a perfect example of self-translation for a good purpose. It successfully displays a certain culture to the Western world in a beautiful literary form. It manifests an alternative yet strongly present society away from the mainstream narrative.

It might not have been an issue for classical authors such as Balzac or Mark Twain or Goethe or the Brontë sisters. They were only working with native speech in the same language. But when a novelist writes in a second language, there are many more layers of self-translation. One of the most difficult exercises is to reconstruct authentic dialogue in English that is supposed to be spoken originally in another language. It is a huge issue for immigrant writers as well as for those who write in languages other than the mainstream European ones.

One of my novels, *UFO in Her Eyes,* bears the traces of that struggle. It was a novel I wrote in English in my early years of living in Britain. Linguistically I was too weak to compose anything sophisticated in English. But I permitted myself to do so, for many reasons. It is a novel set in a backwater Chinese village with peasants speaking crudely and swearing nonstop. In my head, while I was writing in English, every character spoke my hometown dialect or some other dialect close to mine. Of course, the dirty jokes and bitter curses the peasants made in my story were vivid in my head as well as in my ears. I was hearing them all the time in my imagination. But once my hands touched the keyboard I found I was stuck. How should I translate their speech? The English conversation given to my Chinese peasants went through countless revisions. In the beginning, the dialogue sounded strange because I tried to translate the local jokes and casual metaphors into plain English. Most of them did not work. "Cow's cunt" (niu-bi) means something great in Chinese, but not in English. The Chinese expression "Old

Sky" (lao-tian) means "what the hell," but if I use "Old Sky" in English, it does not convey that hellish feeling at all. With each revision, I took out all those direct translations for swear words and idioms and made it "smooth," in other words not metaphors but equivalent English expressions. Still, it did not work. A farmer greeting a butcher with "How are you, mate?" does not sound Chinese. On the other hand, "What the fuck, you have eaten and now you have nothing to do?" is far more realistic for a Chinese story set in a village. In my earlier versions, I didn't get the tone quite right for the village butcher character, as I did not know how to translate him. In a later version, I constructed the conversation around his cultural background, as I did with my other village characters. For example, when the local authority accuses the butcher of not having met the hygiene standards, the butcher defends himself: "I couldn't give a dog's arse what any Food Hygiene Office says!" And then: "Too many flies on my pork? Well, I'll kill them then . . . as I'm sure you know, I'm a Parasite Eradication Hero." The butcher here reminds the officials that during the 1950s he was awarded a medal for his efforts in exterminating sparrows and rats. Therefore he deserves respect. In this translational process, there is no longer a grounding for any notion of "authenticity"; it is all about simulation. All I can remember of writing that book is that I had to construct a unique linguistic realm in my head and on my lips, a hybrid world of speech and meaning. The characters speak neither Chinese nor English but a hybrid language—Xiaolu Guo's broken English. And if Xiaolu Guo's English works in that novel, that is all that matters. It does not matter much if her language works in reality. Writers do not have much reality, having fully committed to a writing life.

But then, I am probably wrong. It is about real life too. How people translate themselves in another culture, how they make themselves understood or appreciated, is important for survival. There is an inherent creativity in our daily communication, in crossing cultures, languages, and different personalities. A mysterious process is going on when we translate or interpret or rewrite a story. All I ask myself in this process is: have I emerged free from the troubled part of the river, and can I see the open water?

In trying to get to the other bank, we must always bear in mind where the shore is on both sides. Translation is the process of swimming from one shore to the other. As you swim, you can see the depths in the water beneath you, with its entangled weeds, hidden reefs, and dangerous eddies. You need to be skilled and sensitive and to know how to preserve yourself. But then, when you have managed to cross the river, the bank you have come from has changed, and you can never quite return.

## *Reading Suggestions*

George Orwell, *Politics and the English Language*

Nathalie Léger, *Suite for Barbara Loden*

V. S. Naipaul, *The Enigma of Arrival*

Jorge Luis Borges, *Selected Non-Fictions*

Shen Fu, *Six Records of a Floating Life*

Li Po and Tu Fu, *Poems*

# On Queerness

*Zeyn Joukhadar*

> To be normal is to be Western European, North American, male, white, middle class, able bodied, and heterosexual, all our attempts at normativity fail. We live in queer failure . . . We drown in boatloads while crossing the Mediterranean and the world carries on without missing a beat. So no, we are not normal. We do not aspire to normalcy.
> —Hugo Canham, "The Water Oriented Away
> from Normativity"

**As a child, I used to believe that novels were first** spoken, then written down once, perfectly. I imagined that being a novelist meant repeating a story to yourself quietly in your room, over and over again, until it was sealed into your memory and you could ink it. I'd heard stories had been passed down like this among my ancestors. I knew people who had memorized and recited the Qur'an by heart, and I knew, if only vaguely, of Arab ways of telling stories that predated the written word.

I learned English primarily from my dad, who stayed home with us while my mom worked. His first language was Arabic, but he spoke English with us. The electrified rail of the English language ran through all our interactions. At school, teachers assumed I was a non-native English speaker; they rooted out words and phrases I'd learned from my dad, particular ways he had of saying things, and did their best to burn them out. Six years old, I'd come home and correct him and be answered with a slap. When he spoke English outside our apartment, he spoke with a measured, formal voice he never used with us, an English that told a story he'd been practicing far longer than I had been alive. That story was both about the English language and about who he was supposed to be inside it. Within the confines and expectations of English, he translated himself for people who used the strictures of language to frame him as an outsider, no matter how well he spoke. America wielded the blade of English to divide us from each other.

Before I knew I was trans, before I had even heard the word, I understood that English, in my father's mouth and in my own, was already queer. Outside the walls of our little studio apartment in New York, white people made it clear that the English I learned from my dad would always be considered failure: a failure to assimilate, to conform, to disappear.

English is my mother tongue, but I speak and write it with a wound inside that doesn't heal. I share versions of this wound with many others: non-native English speakers, speakers of dialects like AAVE (African American Vernacular English), speakers of (or those with ancestors who spoke) Indigenous languages forcibly suppressed by colonialism and genocide—this is only to name a few. In a world and an industry dominated by whiteness, Anglophone writers of color make a conscious choice to use a language in which we don't often have the luxury of feeling safe or understood. Whatever story we set out to tell, we come to the page bracing ourselves against this language that can and will bite the hand that bears the ink. We know that our deviations from white- and Western-centered norms may be framed as failure, rather than craft; we know better than our oppressors the ways the English language may betray us.

Thanks to colonialism, imperialism, and U.S.-centrism, we need not even speak English to be wounded by it. In my foreword to the 2020 Queer + Trans Voices issue of *Mizna*, "Worlds of Our Own Making," I wrote: "Language is deployed to fabricate a history to which we have never belonged, not even when we survived it. Words are borrowed from colonial languages because our lives are painted as untranslatable; when translating into Arabic, 'queer' and 'homosexual' are often left in the original English."

Power seeks always to render itself invisible, so invisible that it doesn't even need to speak to frame a discussion. If I'm forced to spell out the English *queer* as كوير or *trans* as ترانس, then my queer-ness and trans-ness are already difference. They become concepts that can only be located within the linguistic topography of En-glish. Many monolingual English speakers may not even realize the racism of the assumption that queer and trans identities are some-how more at home in English than in Arabic or other languages. The English wedges itself between me and the people I love, posi-tioning my queerness or trans-ness or any other part of me not as innate characteristics—things that could also be part of them—but instead as *other*, as *outside*. There are Arabic alternatives to "queer" or "homosexual"—*mithliyy/a,* for instance, derived from the Arabic word for "same" and meaning gay/lesbian—though many of them, especially those that are reclaimed, are heavy with painful histories. For many of my loved ones, *queer* sounds respectable and academic largely because of its American-ness. To say, instead, the Arabic *khawal* (originally a term denoting a male dancer) or the Italian *frocio*—both more or less meaning "faggot"—hit stingingly close to home precisely because they speak to intimate histories the authorial, sterile English cannot capture. For me to describe my queerness or trans-ness with these reclaimed words is to submit to all the messy, deep-rooted associations I have not only with the words themselves but also with what I grew up believing about myself, my gender, and the place I occupy within these languages, about my place at kitchen tables and on living room couches and in cities in which I will always be perceived as a stranger.

Sometimes I use *queer* to distance myself from these feelings. Sometimes I use it because, when I was growing up, all my models of what it might mean to have a queer or trans life, a queer or trans future, were white American lives, white American futures, white languages of embodiment and possibility. In their introduction to the Trans Futures (6:4) issue of *Trans Studies Quarterly*, Jian Neo Chen and micha cárdenas write that "binary cisgender [is] structured through whiteness." Later in the same issue, V Varun Chaudhry adds that "everything we know about dominant genders—both masculinity and femininity—are based on white bourgeois normativity," and Olivia Fiorilli states that "whiteness is a requisite of transnormativity." This is to say: when I set out to write stories about people who looked and spoke and lived like me, it took years to tune out the messages I'd internalized about what kind of bodies make a story "queer."

I come from a family in which queerness is often understood as something private and unspoken, a culture in which not everything needs to be declared publicly in order to be "valid." Sometimes, this is grounded in a justified fear of further violence from the people who have the power to hurt us. I grew up understanding that my family and I had been assigned certain stories by colonialism, war, authoritarianism, and American racism and Islamophobia. We went to great lengths to make ourselves inconspicuous by adhering to these stories, and for good reason.

As a child, I came to believe that there were certain things that could happen inside of the English I'd been taught in school—and thus inside of whiteness—that could happen nowhere else. To be queer and Arab or trans and Muslim was to be presumed already dead and thus unable to speak for myself. I was rarely allowed to exist beyond the lips of those who held the mic. Within the languages and the stories permitted to me—stories in which my queerness or trans-ness would only be deemed valid if I disavowed my culture, family, faith—only a sliver of me could ever be expressed. And if the heart of what I felt remained unspeakable, then I feared they were right to claim I didn't exist.

Maybe you, dear writer, have feared this, too.

I wish I'd understood earlier that the queerness inherent to my life, my trans and Arab body, and my relationships—like the queerness in my English—is not a limitation but a strength. I think of the page like I think of my body: as a site of possibility. My goal is not necessarily to make the reader understand. My goal is to build an engine that will show the reader how it feels to be alive in a specific moment. Specificity is anything but failure. It is power.

Refusing to explain, of course, comes with challenges. As marginalized writers, most of us are expected, at one point or another, to render ourselves fit for consumption, to spell out for dominant culture readers the ways in which we are like them in order to make them care. The page, like the street or the hospital or the town registrar or even the kitchen table, is a space where gatekeepers often attempt to funnel us into one of two positions: either respectable or silent. I spend a lot of time and effort in my work to resist this binary, and I want to give you, dear writer, some tools and encouragement to do the same.

Kemi Adeyemi's 2019 *Women and Performance* essay "Beyond 90°: The Angularities of Black/Queer/Women/Lean" is a response to Rashaad Newsome's 2012 performance "Shade Compositions," in which a chorus of Black femmes aim gestures and sounds of disapproval, questioning, and anger to the audience without directly stating what they disapprove of. They refuse to explain themselves to the viewer. This kind of physical and vocal "leaning," Adeyemi writes, is a reframing, a refusal to occupy either the "upright" position of respectability or the prone position of those marked for death by the violent logics of the state. To lean is to refuse the binary of success/failure, life/death impressed upon us.

If anger tells us we deserve something better, then maybe leaning can help us make space for our rage without allowing it to dictate the terms of our discussions. Some of my favorite creative works, both written and visual, are those that do this kind of structural reframing in order to make space for our stories: the layering of disparate text and image in Bishakh Som's graphic short story collection *Apsara Engine,* for example, the way the fantastic intrudes on the ordinary in each panel, the way time and narrative fold in on themselves in uncanny ways. Or take the way fa'afafine visual artist Yuki Kihara talks back (literally) to the past in *Paradise Camp:* after "upcycling" the paintings of French painter Paul Gauguin by photographing fa'afafine in the same poses as the paintings, Kihara uses makeup and prosthetics to transform herself into Gauguin in order to talk back to his racism and transphobia, transmuting pain and anger into something beautiful, genius, and delightfully campy. By refusing the strictures of respectability and engaging with our subject matter on our own terms, our work as queer and trans artists is often richer, funnier, and far more interesting.

Let me tell you a story. At the start of my second novel, *The Thirty Names of Night*, the trans protagonist is in the process of choosing a new name. I wanted the reader to linger with him in the limbo of this choice for most of the book, and I wanted them to do so without knowing his deadname. The Western literary canon is full of nameless white male narrators; I saw no reason there couldn't be a trans, Arab, Muslim one.

Still, I was prompted in early drafts to explain the "problem" of this character's deadname to cis readers. At one point, I considered reframing the novel entirely and starting from scratch. It would have been easier to tell the story from the point where my protagonist chooses his new name, setting the story in some triumphant future. *Nadir*, I could have begun, *is an Arabic name meaning "rare."*

But I didn't. I wanted to tell a story about the moment we begin to understand that no one is coming to save us, the moment we understand that no matter what we do, we will have failed someone, somehow, and that this failure is the only path that will bring us to a livable future. Yet I could not disavow the anger I felt toward cis readers' invasive desire to know not only my characters' deadnames but my own. So, as an act of refusal, I left a space at the beginning of each of Nadir's chapters where his deadname would have been, and then I scribbled the name out by hand. The reader's desire for his deadname erased Nadir's power to define himself, so this scribbling out was a counter-erasure, a refusal to argue his respectability. It was a kind of leaning.

At times, the medicine I channeled was not anger but tenderness. In a parallel timeline in *Thirty Names*, a young artist named Laila Z falls in love with another woman in 1930s Syria. Upon immigrating to New York City's Little Syria neighborhood, she tries to process their brief relationship, gradually realizing that her unmarried aunt, too, is in love with the widow who lives next door. She watches them keep pigeons together, hang laundry together on the tenement roof. Her gaze is tender: unlike the eyes of the white Americans who come to her neighborhood to gawk and to consume, Laila is able to perceive the love between these women and their quiet, private joy. Their relationship is never acknowledged publicly, never spoken of openly, and yet it exists in relatively plain view. The widow eventually passes away, leaving her pigeons to her lover, and maybe everyone knows and maybe no one knows, and no one says a thing.

I didn't write this story to make white, Western readers understand. I didn't write it to invite their savior fantasies. Do they think we were all straight before colonization, as though queerness were a commodity packaged for export? No. I wrote the love stories in *Thirty Names* because when I looked in the mirror at fourteen and thought *No one can ever know that I am this,* my actual fear was *The language I have will never be enough to hold me.* Not because my loved ones wouldn't have understood *queer* or *trans,* but because every time I entered a queer space and encountered racism or Islamophobia or looked for queer books in libraries and found only white characters, I received the message loud and clear that those words were for white people and white experiences. I could use them,

sure, but they would always worm their way into my wounds, itch-
ing like loneliness.

I'm not saying I haven't found solace in those words or that they
don't or can't describe us. But I am saying that to write anything as
a queer or trans writer of color is to refuse to allow oneself to be
shoved quietly out of view. It is to be angry nearly all the time and to
find ways of transmuting that rage into something usable. It is to
insist that what we feel need not be translated. My father once wrote
of his anger, "The bull comes out of its hide," and he meant both
cave and skin. Longing for the taste of home, I ask my lover to port
me Syrian za'atar, and a ship sighs into the harbor of my tongue.
Just as it was for my father, all my other languages are always present in my English, dislodging and disorienting it, jarring open space
for me to dwell inside. I disrupt my languages because I want the
perfect understanding that exists on the other side of them, as
though I might have a map for living if only I could hold each un-
languaged sensation in my hand like an egg, if only I could make my
words transparent enough that I could see myself through their
knit.

Toni Morrison said, "I stood at the border, stood at the edge, and
claimed it as central. Claimed it as central, and let the rest of the
world move over to where I was." Torrey Peters, who won the 2021
PEN/Hemingway Award for her novel *Detransition, Baby,* has written
and spoken about how trans people writing for other trans people
makes for better stories, because to explain the conditions of trans
life to cis people forces us to oversimplify and overexplain. To write
about the conditions of your life for an audience like you requires
you to tell your audience something they don't already know, which
pushes you to better your art. Refusing to tell flattened stories re-

quires us to dream beyond the limited possibilities given to us by cisheteronormativity and whiteness. Put another way in another context, I often come back to a quote by Sophia Azeb, writing of Palestinian futures in *The Funambulist:* "How we make meaning of ourselves and our being as Palestinian when we are no longer beholden to understanding ourselves in the shadows of disaster is not just a passing whim, a theoretical exercise. To ask how and who we are now and who we will be when we are free insists that our future-selves are always in sight, that our freedom is always in sight."

I used to believe in that perfect, rigid novel, written down once in pristine rapture. But if I've written and rewritten this letter to you more than a dozen times, dear writer, it's because I now understand that envisioning ourselves when we are free is a recursive, collective process. I don't know who we will be when we are free, but I do believe in freedom that feels expansive, one with space for my every part and facet. White cis people often try to frame me as divided, as though my emotions, sensations, and experiences don't coexist in my body all the time. My queerness is a Muslim queerness; my trans embodiment is an Arab one. They are indivisible. Over the course of my career, I've learned to relinquish the mirage of the universal in favor of the specific, the complex, and the multiplicitous. The important thing is not to write a story for everyone; rather, the goal is to be vividly alive to myself and to the world. *Universal* is a locked door, an all-white room. I do not live my life in rooms like that. I come to the page with my loved ones' queer languages in my ear, my protagonist's scribbled-out name in my hand, armed with the intimacies I know so well I could recite them by heart. I pearl them in my mouth. I tell myself I don't have to get it right the first time, that I don't have to envision my freedom in a single, swift gulp. I resolve to speak my freedom into being again and again, until the language rolls over and bellies itself to my touch, until something joyful springs from my tongue.

## Reading Suggestions

b binaohan, *decolonizing trans/gender 101*

Hugo Canham, "The Water Oriented Away from Normativity," *Africa Is a Country,* available at africasacountry.com/2022/01/the-water-oriented-away-from-normativity

Alexander Chee, *How to Write an Autobiographical Novel*

Tom Cho, *Look Who's Morphing*

Audre Lorde, *Sister Outsider*

Toni Morrison, *The Source of Self-Regard*

Jasbir K. Puar, *Terrorist Assemblages: Homonationalism in Queer Times*

Bishakh Som, *Apsara Engine*

# On Telling and Showing

Jamil Jan Kochai

**My first novel began almost by accident.**

Its plot was rooted in a memory from when I was a twelve-year-old boy. One summer day, my mother's family's guard dog, Budabash, broke out of his heavy iron chain, leaped over the twelve-foot-high walls of our clay compound, and escaped out onto the American-occupied roads of Logar. My uncles and cousins and I went after him. Inspired by these memories, I wrote the first draft of a short story. But I soon realized that there were other characters and histories and plotlines that needed their own time in the spotlight. The form of a short story wouldn't be able to contain them all. And so began the mysterious process of figuring out how I was going to tell the tale of 99 Nights in Logar.

Based upon the edicts I had learned from creative writing classes and craft books in college (thou shalt not use the passive voice, thou shalt not underestimate the intelligence of your reader, thou shalt not "tell"), I assumed that my novel had to be propelled by action or character choice and that it largely needed to be conveyed through scene. In other words, I needed my characters to be actors, and I needed my story to be shown. In the beginning, this seemed simple enough. I sent my characters (Marwand, Zia, Gul, and Da-wood) out onto the roads of Logar in search of their dangerous guard dog, and I had them act! The boys arranged ambushes and threw stones and prayed and interrogated neighbors and got into arguments, and almost all of this action occurred within scene. I wanted my readers to see the village, to experience the mischief. But soon I ran into trouble.

The problem was backstory. I was having a difficult time incor-porating all of the familial, communal, and national histories I thought were necessary for the telling of my tale. The secret trage-dies and love affairs in my characters' backgrounds. The massacres and atrocities buried beneath the roads of the village. The three de-cades of almost constant warfare in Afghanistan. These events not only shaped my characters' pasts; they were also actively shaping how my characters lived from day to day, moment to moment. In many ways, the present conditions of my characters' lives were de-termined by the American Occupation, which was a response to the 9/11 attacks, which were conducted by allies of the Taliban, who had come to power because of the mujahideen civil wars, which was a result of the disastrous Soviet occupation of Afghani-stan in 1979. These historical threads were critical to the fictional world I was building, a world that existed in the shadow of my par-ents' memory of Afghanistan (a village at peace) that was lost to war. Yet there didn't seem to be enough space between my action-oriented scenes to incorporate these crucial histories. When I did find room for a bit of backstory, it often felt contrived.

I was held back by a learned aversion to summary and exposi-tion. I'd write a passage of backstory or historical information and then immediately cut it out again for the sake of "the scene." I kept having the boys find more trouble and create more problems until the plot got so heavy it ground to a halt and the momentum of the chase fizzled out. I had written myself into a corner. Beneath a mulberry tree in the middle of the village, Gul was lost, Dawood had passed out, Zia was having a crisis of faith, and Marwand didn't know what to do about any of it.

Even worse: neither did I.

I stopped writing for months. It was horrifying. I had been so myopically focused on pace and momentum that when I found myself stuck on plot, I couldn't figure how to write myself out of the problem.

I recalled a quote by Kafka: "You do not need to leave your room. Remain sitting at your table and listen. Do not even listen, simply wait, be quiet, still and solitary. The world will freely offer itself to you to be unmasked, it has no choice, it will roll in ecstasy at your feet."

So I sat. I listened. I waited.

But Logar did not roll in ecstasy at my feet.

The boys were being stubborn. Or maybe they were just frightened into paralysis.

Whatever it was, I decided to take a break. I did what I always do in moments of writerly distress. I read. And, Alhamdullilah, I ended up coming upon a book on my shelf that I had been meaning to read for several years. As if it were ordained by Allah, I discovered the solution to my problem in *The Arabian Nights*.

Almost immediately, I felt utterly compelled by the complex web of internal stories through which *The Arabian Nights* is constructed. The stories within stories act as confessions, jokes, historical accounts, gossip, digressions, tricks, seduction, and prophecies.

They have a marvelous way of both compressing time and providing background while centering the act of oral storytelling itself.

For example, *The Arabian Nights* begins with the famous frame narrative of young Shahrazad's attempt to outwit King Shahrayar, who plans to murder her in the morning, by telling him a story at night. Her first tale is about a merchant attacked by a demon. She beguiles him with the narrative, but at the moment of highest tension, as the demon raises his sword to strike, Shahrazad pauses her narration because morning has arrived. She promises to continue the tale at night, and King Shahrayar, "burning with curiosity to hear the rest," allows Shahrazad to live until the conclusion of her tale. Shahrazad, therefore, employs a form of narrative suspense that keeps both the story and herself alive.

On the second night, Shahrazad continues her tale, relating how the merchant convinces the demon to allow him to live for one more year in order to discharge his obligations. An entire year passes within a few paragraphs as the merchant says his goodbyes and pays his dues. True to his word, the merchant then returns to the orchard where he met the demon and is approached by an old man who inquires about his situation. On hearing the merchant's story, the old man, like King Shahrayar, is so intrigued that he too is determined to wait until he sees its conclusion.

On the third night, Shahrazad tells the king that the merchant is approached by two more old men who also want to witness how events turn out. Shortly afterward, the demon returns and tells the merchant to prepare himself for death. But, again, morning overtakes Shahrazad, and it is only on the fourth night that we, like King Shahrayar, see one of the three old men sitting with the merchant challenge the demon to a wager: if his story is more incredible than the story of the demon, then the demon must relinquish a third of his claim over the merchant. We are then presented with the first story within a story within the frame narrative. That the old man's tale is being told to save the life of the merchant—just as Shahrazad's story is being told to save her own life—only adds to the metafictional quality of *The Arabian Nights*.

The three old men are each given a chance to tell a short tale from their own lives. Thus, within a few pages, we are given the backstories (decades of personal histories) of multiple characters. The frame narrative launches into an oral narrative that contains yet another oral narrative, thereby collapsing multiple levels of time (Shahrazad's nights with King Shahrayar, the merchant's year-long journey away from and back to the demon, and the old man's encounter with his son, who has turned into a bull).

These narrative techniques seemed utterly fantastic but also deeply familiar. That is to say, it was through *The Arabian Nights* that I began to think back to the way that my parents and aunts and grandparents often told stories within stories, stories without endings, stories with digressions, and stories with extended histories. For instance, in 2017, during my second year at graduate school, my father told me a story about a phone call he received in 1996 from a cousin in Afghanistan he thought had died many years earlier. When my father asked his cousin how he had survived the war(s) in Afghanistan, his cousin told him a story about how, in 1984, he was captured in Badakhshan by a murderous militia, whose commander, while interrogating the captive, happened to recognize the name of my family's home village. My father's cousin asked the commander how he knew about a little village in Logar and the commander told him a story from 1981, in which the commander had deserted his post as a communist soldier and my father had hidden him in his home for several months, thereby saving his life. The commander then released my father's cousin to repay the old debt.

At the time, this seemed like a fantastic series of coincidences, but my father assured me that it was the will of Allah. His cousin was destined to meet the commander my father had saved all those years ago because it had not been written for him to die in a prison cell. Many of my parents' stories centered the will of Allah in this manner.

Similarly, in *The Arabian Nights*, "God" or "fate" is allowed to take part in the narrative in a way that I hadn't seen very much in contemporary American fiction, which, to me, always places a great emphasis upon agency and action and psychological ruminations. But in *The Arabian Nights*, events occurred as they occurred, one event generating the next, due to prophecies and destinies and by the will of Allah, and it was all woven together so intricately and so beautifully that I felt inspired by the method. Certainly, at times, it came at the cost of the agency of the characters and the immediacy of the scenes. But I didn't see why my novel couldn't meld both forms of storytelling. A story driven by "agency" *and* "fate." A story that is both "shown" *and* "told." A story with stories within it.

When I returned at last to my novel, instead of forcing my characters to act, I allowed them, for a few pages, to behave passively. "Fate" was thrown into the mix, and I sent them a few storytellers to get them out of their jam. From that point on, instead of seeking out the next action or scene, I looked for the next story, the next storyteller.

By incorporating a multiplicity of voices into the text, I could create a more complex vision of my parents' home village in Logar, with all its political, sociological, and historical dimensions. I was able to compress time and provide histories in a manner that felt organic to the themes of the novel. At one point, for example, as Marwand's relatives are all sitting together and drinking tea in 2005, I was able to have them tell stories from the Soviet War in the 1980s, the civil wars in the 1990s, and the early stages of the U.S. invasion in 2001, thereby demonstrating how one historical event led to the next and how each of these violent catastrophes dramatically shaped the lives of my characters.

Of course, all these stories within stories necessitated a great deal of "telling" or summarization, and while I became more comfortable with this method, I still felt irked by the need to emphasize scene. I then turned to another deeply influential book: *One Hundred Years of Solitude* by Gabriel García Márquez, which, with its emphasis on oral storytelling, fate, circularity, and magic, seems to owe a great deal to *The Arabian Nights*.

When I first read *One Hundred Years of Solitude*, I was left in awe of what a story could accomplish in just a few hundred pages. Macondo—the little adobe village that suffers revolutions, massacres, and capitalist exploitation—reminded me so much of my parents' home village in Logar that *One Hundred Years of Solitude* became the pinnacle of all that I hoped to achieve with my own work. And yet, returning to the novel with a specific eye for its use of scene, I found that García Márquez, as he propelled the reader through the history of the village, didn't write very many "scenes" in the strict sense of the term.

García Márquez's dialogue is sparse. Characters don't have long confrontational conversations or interactions. They fall in love, have their hearts broken, join revolutions, become disillusioned by war, survive executions, and lose all sense of reality within a chapter or two. Despite its reliance on summary, *One Hundred Years of Solitude* maintains a wonderful, lifelike, and exhilarating vibrancy in its movement from one page, one chapter, one war, one life, and one generation to the next. García Márquez accomplishes this feat by writing summaries that are chock-full of precise and unexpected images and details.

Take this passage, with italics added:

They went down along the *stony bank of the river* to the place where years before they had found the soldier's armor, and from there they went *into the woods along a path between wild orange trees.* At the end of the first week they killed and roasted a deer, but they agreed to eat only half of it and salt the rest for the days that lay ahead. With that precaution they tried to postpone the necessity of having to eat macaws, *whose blue flesh had a harsh and musky taste.* Then, for more than ten days, they did not see the sun again. *The ground became soft and damp, like volcanic ash,* and the vegetation was thicker and thicker, and *the cries of the birds and the uproar of the monkeys became more and more remote, and the world became eternally sad.* The men on the expedition felt overwhelmed by their most ancient memories in that *paradise of dampness and silence,* going back to before original sin, *as their boots sank into pools of steaming oil and their machetes destroyed bloody lilies and golden salamanders.* For a week, almost without speaking, they went ahead like sleepwalkers *through a universe of grief, lighted only by the tenuous reflection of luminous insects, and their lungs were overwhelmed by a suffocating smell of blood.*

Almost an entire month's worth of adventure is summarized for us over the course of seven sentences, but García Márquez makes certain that even as the reader is being rapidly moved through time, they are still immersed in an abundance of specific, physical, visual, and sensual elements. He balances instances of abstraction (the world becoming "eternally sad" or the "universe of grief") with concrete details, thereby allowing the physical and the conceptual to play off each other. It's a tactic he uses consistently and effectively throughout his novel. In this way, even as García Márquez hurtles us through summaries, his reader is still able to envision the yellow flowers that rain on the streets of Macondo after the death of José Arcadio Buendía. They smell the scent of rosewater that wafts from José Arcadio's (the 2nd) hair as he wanders about his home. They hear the patter of the torrential rains that fall on Macondo for four years, eleven months, and two days. These images and details (carefully chosen and beautifully depicted) allow García Márquez to "show" through his "telling." There is no dichotomy between summary and scene. Rather, García Márquez is able to fuse both techniques so that the narrative of *One Hundred Years of Solitude* compresses a great deal of time but still allows the reader to linger upon particularly crucial and vibrant images, sights, sounds, experiences, and feelings. This is part of what makes *One Hundred Years of Solitude* a feat of storytelling, and it's what I attempted to incorporate in my own passages of summary in *99 Nights in Logar*.

As I continued drafting my novel, I became better attuned to seeking stories not only within the text but also outside it. Oftentimes, when I returned home to speak with my parents about their memories of Logar, I noticed all the beautiful ways in which they complicated and deepened their stories: their details and pauses, their stuttering and misremembering, their digressions and humor, how they spoke faster when happy and slower when saddened, the manner in which the historical seemed to meld with the mythological, the sheer amount of time (decades of war!) they could subsume within a five-minute tale, and the way that they omitted the most obvious information to focus on a single, telling image—the pale hue of henna etched on a severed finger or the echoing of a voice in the mountains. With time, I realized that the kernels of all that I loved about literature were already contained within their oral narratives. These stories were always "told" to me, and it was precisely this realization that allowed me to return to my work with the liberating knowledge that a story could be "told" just as artfully as it could be "shown."

## Reading Suggestions

Joan Silber, *The Art of Time in Fiction: As Long as It Takes*

Elena Ferrante, *My Brilliant Friend*, translated by
    Ann Goldstein

Toni Morrison, *Beloved*

Justin Torres, *We the Animals*

Leo Tolstoy, *Hadji Murat*, translated by Richard Pevear
    and Larissa Volokhonsky

Gabriel García Márquez, *Chronicle of a Death Foretold*,
    translated by Gregory Rabassa

Brooks Landon, *Building Great Sentences: How to Write
  the Kinds of Sentences You Love to Read*
Patrick Chamoiseau, *Texaco*, translated by Rose-Myriam
  Réjouis and Val Vinokurov
Daniyal Mueenuddin, *In Other Rooms, Other Wonders*
Sandra Cisneros, *Woman Hollering Creek and Other Stories*
Isabel Allende, *The House of the Spirits*, translated by
  Magda Bogin

# On the Inactive Protagonist

*Vida Cruz-Borja*

**Let me take you through the anatomy of an active** protagonist, one that everyone can relate to. We'll make our protagonist—we'll call him "John"—young and healthy, male, of humble origins (perhaps he's from a farming village). But his status will not be humble for long, for John is dreaming of greatness someday, or of adventuring across the world, or perhaps of winning the heart of the most beautiful princess throughout the faux-medieval European continent he hails from. He'll encounter myriad obstacles and antagonists along the way, but since he's worked so hard from the bottom up, you know for sure he'll get what he wants by the end of the story.

For John isn't just a protagonist—he's a hero, a Chosen One. He's gotta be rewarded for single-handedly saving the world, after all (nothing the right weapon couldn't fix). There is no god, natural or supernatural phenomenon, technology, society, or man that cannot be beaten and tamed by John's sword. Not even himself.

I never said he was white. I didn't need to. This description of John, albeit bare-bones, plays into the default assumption readers have of the heroes of these kinds of stories. The less specific his description, the more you can project how close he is to the default. But what gives his race away isn't his name or the amalgamation of where he's from. It's his almost fluid mobility toward his "destiny." The same mobility that deems him an "active protagonist" in the eyes of a certain kind of reader.

This is a mobility that is not afforded to anyone who isn't young, healthy and able, neurotypical, middle-class, white, cis, straight, and/or male.

Now imagine that John's obstacles, his conflicts, are a mountain. He can come at that mountain with a sword or a magic staff or an army or bombs—it doesn't matter as long as he can get over it, around it, under it, through it, in order to reach his goal.

But what if his conflicts, his obstacles, are other people?

Every time this mountain is represented by a tribe of nonwhite people threatening to throw John into a volcano for the sake of a savage god; by a woman refusing to give him sex; by people coded queer or trans in their villainous behavior; by someone with a tragic backstory rooted in the loss of a body part or a mental disorder or abuse; by a blue-collar worker who turned to terrorism out of desperation—every time these "characterizations" are used, it reinforces that what is not default is to be beaten. Conquered. Killed.

Now let's flip the script. Let me take you through the anatomy of characters who are commonly labeled "inactive protagonist."

They are marginalized in some way, via race or class or gender or sex or ability. They will most certainly have suffered some kind of trauma (or three, or more), whether physical, emotional, psychological, or sexual. These two things have inevitably and inextricably colored not only how they perceive and navigate the world they live in but also how gods, natural or supernatural phenomena, technology, society, or other people react to *them*.

The latter, especially, is not something they can control. Not when you live in a world that wasn't made for you. Not when *you have no choice but to live* in a world that wasn't made for you.

Make any one of these people the protagonist. They become the mountain, and John and whoever and whatever he brings with him becomes a wave. Wave after wave of conflict and violence. This kind of protagonist is not going anywhere because their circumstances, their lack of mobility, keep them rooted to the spot, unable to take the wave head-on. But they keep standing because it is either survival or annihilation.

This is also a valid way of presenting a character's agency in fiction.

What do you do when co-workers gossip about your sexual activities when you file a case against a boss who touched you without your consent?

You survive.

What do you do when your parents throw you out of the house permanently because you dared kiss someone of the same sex?

You survive.

What do you do when your serotonin-deprived brain repeats daily the mantra that you are worthless, undeserving of the love of others?

You survive.

What do you do when a hostile country rains bombs around your house?

You survive.

What do you do when a pandemic rages and you cannot leave your house and your leaders have very little empathy and political will to educate on and distribute vaccines?

You survive.

In any way you can, even if it means staying put, even if it means taking cover somewhere, even if it means enduring a bad situation, you survive.

And not in the callous "oh, you'll live" kind of way, but in an "I will hold on even though I am raw and bleeding and out of anything to give because the only other option is the abyss" kind of way.

These are not problems that go away if you shake the right weapon at them. In fiction, it would feel cheap if a character could just swing their sword or wave their magic staff and *poof*, problem solved. No decent person would dare call people who survive these situations "inactive." So why are characters called such when they choose to survive in fiction?

I see it all the time as a developmental editor. A BIPOC writer with one last fuck to give will come to me with their manuscript— often a competent and highly original story doing something new with world-building or structure or form—and their beta readers' comments, most of which are some refrain of "your protagonist doesn't have any agency" or "your protagonist is just reacting to the plot instead of driving it" or "things just keep happening to your protagonist, they need more agency."

The writer will ask me, "Could you read with an eye to see if that's actually the case and tell me what I can do to improve?"

A suspicion forms in my mind, and I just *have* to voice it: "By any chance, were your beta readers white?"

Every time, the answer is a resounding yes.

What is perceived as "activeness" in a character manifests the American values of rugged individualism, of "pull yourself up by the bootstraps," of Manifest Destiny. "Activeness" in character, as promoted by the U.S. publishing industry, ignores the contribution and influence of community and society on the personality and actions of the character.

Much of classical and contemporary literature and comics from both East and West is full of protagonists who simply observe (*The Great Gatsby*), who survive bleak or volatile circumstances (*Beloved, The Unbearable Lightness of Being*), who have no choice but to navigate the political sea around them at great cost (*The Remarried Empress*). But there is a strange insistence from contemporary U.S. publishing to make characters in science fiction and fantasy "do something that affects the plot." It demands that marginalized writers imagine characters with a mobility that they themselves do not have, resulting in characters that feel untrue to the writers but somehow fit a narrow vision of "marketability."

If you look at it a certain way, however, most stories are about characters solving problems. And while there are indeed books featuring marginalized characters solving problems with a "Western" sense of agency (*The Poppy War*), there should be more books that feature marginalized people solving problems that differ from the way people of the default do. Perhaps, then, we need to reframe our relationship to conflict.

This is not, by the way, a diatribe against conflict. It works perfectly in tandem with a three-act structure. But not every story is served well by the three-act structure. And a character can experience conflicts without resolving these with a competition mindset, an us-versus-them way of thinking—in other words, if you keep using a sword, everything will look like something to strike. In fact, you can write an entire story without using conflict to generate drama, but that is another essay altogether.

You could kill a villain to solve a problem, but that is only a short-term solution and may not be true to the heart of your story. Your characters could solve problems through community building, through mercy and forgiveness, through acceptance of uncontrollable circumstances, through uniting and reuniting other characters, through reparations. Even through fleeing or through staying put.

Here's the thing about mountains. No matter what is thrown at one, it keeps standing. Marginalized peoples often don't realize it, but we have the strength of mountains. We actively overcome obstacles with the decision to stand our ground instead of charging in.

We are the mountain. And we are not going anywhere.

## Reading Suggestions

Matthew Salesses, *Craft in the Real World: Rethinking Fiction Writing and Workshopping*

Felicia Rose Chavez, *The Anti-Racist Writing Workshop: How to Decolonize the Creative Classroom*

Elaine Castillo, *How to Read Now: Essays*

Kiini Ibura Salaam, *On Finding Your Voice: Notes from the Trenches*

Nisi Shawl and Cynthia Ward, *Writing the Other: A Practical Approach*

Aidan Doyle, editor, *The Writer's Book of Doubt*

Ursula K. Le Guin, *Dancing at the Edge of the World*

Charlie Jane Anders, *Never Say You Can't Survive*

Cherríe Moraga and Gloria Anzaldúa, editors, *This Bridge Called My Back: Writings by Radical Women of Color*

Paisley Rekdal, *Appropriate: A Provocation*

# On Crime Fiction

*Femi Kayode*

1.

**A week before the publication of my debut novel,**
*Lightseekers*, I was forwarded a review from a respected trade magazine. The content was disheartening: "Though Kayode creates occasional suspense . . . the story fails to gel. Those curious about
Nigerian culture and politics will be most satisfied." The reviewer
seemed as disdainful of my work as they were at the idea of anyone
being "curious" about the culture and politics of my home country.
But that was not all. The reviewer also asserted that I was the pseudonym of a British writer whose only connection to me is that we
are friends on Facebook. How ironic that a reviewer who judged my
novel so authoritatively was unable to get my identity right. My per-
sonhood was erased with the same wanton arrogance as my debut
effort was written off. The mistake has since been corrected, but the
review remains on the landing pages of several prominent online
retailers, underlining the fact that the publication is a preeminent
voice in determining what good storytelling should be.

This singular experience has stayed with me. The dismissal cut
deeper than the euphoria of positive reviews by other major publi-

cations. Perhaps it had to do with my own insecurities as a debut author or the need to have my novel understood and appreciated as a valid contribution to the crime fiction genre. I reflected on the phrase "those curious about Nigerian culture and politics will be most satisfied." I convinced myself that given the emerging nature of crime fiction as a genre in Africa, the reviewer's exposure to works from my part of the world must be limited at best. This conclusion gave me peace. It was not a defense mechanism but rather an affirmation that the reviewer was not my intended audience for *Lightseekers*.

## 2.

Before I was a novelist, I was a middle-aged man at a career crossroads. Well into my forties, I no longer knew where I was going and what I wanted to do. My search for relevance led to a renewed purpose (and pleasure) in reading.

I went back to the books of my youth: the crime novels that entertained me and stirred my imagination. I reconnected with my love for Sidney Sheldon, rediscovered the magic of Stephen King, reveled in the debauchery of Harold Robbins and relived the heart-thumping excitement of the Bourne series. I also searched for Nigerian crime novels that combined literary craftsmanship with a layered illustration of contemporary African life, but they were rare. Most of the novels existed in the "literary" genre, with few authors writing within the crime fiction space.

To explain this observation, I assumed that the genre's association with escapist entertainment was at a dissonance with the expectations of a mostly Western reading audience. These readers have come to expect stories that focus on a crime, with fast-paced action that takes certain aspects of the detection and solving of the crime for granted. An audience exposed to an overwhelming number of procedural TV shows (the *CSI* franchise comes to mind) can be forgiven for having little patience for crime fiction that spends a significant portion of text explaining *why* as a way of providing context. Who has the time to understand the link between the underfunding of tertiary institutions in Africa and the lack of law enforcement units dedicated to profiling offenders on the continent? How would showing the connection between a chaotic national data collection system and the lack of a viable fingerprinting database in Nigeria enrich the enjoyment of the reader?

Another possible reason for the relative dearth of crime fiction in Africa (compared to other literary genres) might be attributed to what the reading audience has come to expect literary work from the continent to entail. Apparently, there is an expectation that the "African novel" will reflect the realities presented in international news media (see the late Binyavanga Wainaina's seminal essay, "How to Write about Africa"). Disease, famine, environmental degradation, postcolonial strife—subjects whose treatment can often come off as "poverty porn"—permeate a lot of what is considered "African writing." Themes outside of these preconceived notions about the continent tend to be deemed "unserious" or unworthy of literary merit.

This sentiment appears to be reinforced by the category under which nearly all literary work by African writers (including those in the diaspora) is placed in bookshops on the continent and in most parts of the world. Irrespective of genre, you'll find works by writers of African origin under "African Fiction" or "African Writing." This is particularly disconcerting when the shelf space for "Fiction" is so far away from the "African Writing" section that one is forced to wonder why the distinction is needed. And if such distinctions should be made, what defines the work as "African"? The author's origins? Where the story is set? I was filled with questions.

3.

*If there's a book you want to read, but it hasn't been written yet, then* **you must write it**.

Toni Morrison's words trailed me as I scanned bookshops in Namibia, where I live; in South Africa, which I visit often for work; and Nigeria, my home country. I searched for crime novels that reflected my reality as a modern African man of Nigerian heritage. I wanted crime novels that would give me the thrill I remembered from my younger years. But this time, I wanted those stories to be about me, my world, and my lived experiences. I wanted crime fiction that captured the complexity of my reality in a way that I couldn't find on shelves—and in a way that mainstream global news media didn't either. I wanted to read about a murder on the streets of Lagos, a car chase in Abuja, a hostage situation in Warri, or a gun fight in Abeokuta. I wanted to explore subterfuge in Accra, a pipeline explosion in Guinea, and a hijacking in the Kenyan airspace.

When I couldn't find enough stories like these, I decided to take Ms. Morrison's advice.

4.

I went back to school.

My first week as a postgraduate student in Creative Writing (with a specialization in Crime Fiction) felt like a homecoming. I was with a dozen other writers in my age group; we were all travelers of sorts, searching for self and meaning. Some might have considered us self-indulgent, going back to school so late in life.

But that was where the similarities ended.

I am a Black man, living and working in Africa. My lived experience was far removed from those of my fellow students and lecturers, who were all European and white and mostly lived in the U.K. As we pitched stories, shared ideas, and tried to hone our voices as writers, it became clear that I had no precedent on which to base my dream of bringing the rich complexity of my world into crime fiction. This is not to say there are no African writers in the crime genre, but I didn't know of them at that time. I looked through the reading list for the course, hoping to find a writer of African origin. None. Apart from Walter Mosley's *Devil in a Blue Dress* and Marlon James's *A Brief History of Seven Killings* (both featuring only as "recommended reading"), there were no writers of color on the list.

As I read my way through the books on the list, few added to my knowledge and understanding of the worlds in which they were set. To my mind, it seemed that a murder in New York could be easily transplanted to Manchester, and one wouldn't miss a beat. A terrorist plot in Paris could very well have happened in Sydney. Few texts contextualized the plots, despite rich and textured settings. I understood little about the sociopolitical environment that allowed the crime to happen. I found few linkages to the historical underpinnings that drove characters to do what they did, except within the subgenre of historical crime fiction that mandated this as a deliverable.

In class, discussions around this observation almost always moved to crime fiction as *entertainment,* as if anything that detracted from this purpose was not true to the genre. This trend confounded me. For instance, my lived experience *demanded* that crime writing could not be divorced from my country's colonial past. How could I write a story that did not take into account the immense lack of infrastructure that facilitated the peculiarities of the crimes that exist in my world? From corruption to political intrigue to murder and more, our crimes are rooted in history, informed by environment, and driven by systemic challenges. How could I entertain without giving context? How could I *authentically* present my world in fiction devoid of the cultural nuances that make it unique?

My early story ideas came across as if they belonged, at best, in the pitch sessions at a school of journalism. I wanted to write about how the endemic corruption in Nigeria is fueled by a dysfunctional political system. I wanted to explore the issues around the ongoing police brutality in my country. I toyed with the idea of writing a story around the environmental concerns in the oil-rich Niger Delta of Nigeria. But the context required to appreciate my story ideas resulted in expositions rather than the propulsive action that is the basis of an effective crime story. The imperative for entertainment got lost in whatever issue I was trying to highlight.

**5.**

Prior to studying Crime Writing, I had obtained a postgraduate diploma in Futures Studies, where I encountered the concept of Systems Thinking. Generally, there are two types of systems: natural and designed. Natural systems refer to living systems whose origins are based on the forces and events of evolution. Designed systems are created, wholly fabricated from scratch to serve a purpose, but can also be a combination of physical construction and nature, such as a solar plant. Systems can also be conceptual or based on human activity.

Systems Thinking is therefore a holistic approach of analysis that focuses on the way a system's constituent parts interrelate and how systems work over time within the context of larger systems. It is fundamentally different from traditional forms of analysis that focus on separating the object of study into its individual pieces.

Every time I consider my country, Nigeria, the first word that comes to mind is "complex." More than 200 million people spread across a vast landscape that ranges from mangrove forests to bare desert, with about 250 ethnic groups speaking close to 500 languages. A country rich in resources but poor in infrastructure. An African nation that had barely recovered from the trauma of colonization before being plunged into one of the bloodiest civil wars in modern history. Add political instability, ethnic tensions, weak institutions, and an outdated constitution inherited from colonial masters, and my home country is the very definition of complexity. Because Systems Thinking offers an effective way to consider the most difficult of problems—those involving complex issues, with a great dependence on the past or the actions of others—I felt it was the perfect tool with which to approach writing a crime novel set in Nigeria.

## 6.

One of the texts we studied in the Crime Fiction program was *In Cold Blood* by Truman Capote. I was fascinated by how this story was unique to the midcentury American zeitgeist and impressed by how its world, despite being alien to me, felt real and tangible. I *understood* it. As I set out to write my own novel, I searched for inspiration in a true crime story that could test the Systems Thinking framework. The optimal story would allow me to unpack the foundations of a society by illustrating how parts of the "system" facilitated the crime and then hindered or presented opportunities for solving the crime.

I found it in the public lynching of four undergraduates in a Nigerian university town, which had shocked the world and sparked widespread outrage. For me, this gruesome event raised far-reaching questions. Why were so few people arrested for the crime despite their identification on numerous videos uploaded on social media? How could this happen? How did we get here as a society?

Drawing on my understanding of Systems Thinking, I divided my questions into the following sections: Political, Economic, Social, Technological, Environmental, and Legal (PESTEL). Before a fellow writer reads this and rolls their eyes at this rather scientific approach to a creative process, I must point out that I had no story at this stage. No characters. No locale. What I had was an incident that I had *intentionally* chosen to inspire what I hoped would emerge as a social crime story. I was just putting my research within a framework for analysis. There was nothing "creative" at this point.

My research revealed that the four victims (in the real-life crime) were accused of being robbers. I asked: what gave this accusation enough credibility to galvanize a mob? This question fell under "social" and demanded further investigation into the town's past experience with armed robbers. That the mobsters felt their actions were just and had posted the crime-in-progress on social media was explored under the relationship of the society with "technology." Discovering that several years after the crime was committed, the case was still in court, and no one had been convicted (as of then), demanded further exploration under a "legal" framework. And so on.

I admit it was a rabbit hole of data gathering, but drawing causal loops between events revealed that I had a complex idea filled with intriguing possibilities.

The next step was to fashion a story around this event. That was when the creative mind was allowed free rein. As this was not a true crime novel, I had to identify the points of departure in my story from the real-life crime. Functionally, it would have been difficult to explore four victims adequately, so I settled for three. I recreated the crime scene in a fictional university town, which allowed me a lot of latitude in crafting scenarios. I built a story world using the information gleaned with my PESTEL model and created characters whose actions correlated with the factors I had identified as the driving forces that made the crime possible.

I wanted to use the real-life crime as inspiration and move beyond it in my fiction. But it was also important to pay homage to the misery the tragedy had brought on the boys' families and, indeed, the community itself. I conducted interviews and scoured articles about the victims' families and came to a firm conviction: human emotions like pain or grief as a response to tragedy are universal. The collective human experience was sufficient inspiration to create characters that were real and bore little or no similarities to the family members of the victims in the real-life crime. I must admit, having a degree in psychology also came in handy here.

Looking back, there is nothing novel about my approach—if I had a dollar for every crime writer who was inspired by a story they came across in the newspapers!—but it was my intentional application of Systems Thinking toward the synthesis of my research that enriched the context I felt the reader needed.

## 7.

There were times when the weight of the research and my convoluted approach threatened to block my progress. I pulled through because I chose to employ those conflicting emotions in my writing. When I felt anger about what I was discovering, I made my protagonist just as mad. When I felt depressed by the state of affairs about the real case (the trial was ongoing at the time I was writing the book), I transmitted that negativity to the story. In a sense, the process became cathartic. The deeper I was willing to dig, the easier it was for me to project my impressions and feelings onto the story. The research grounded me, but it was the characters who inspired me.

A much-discussed burden on the writer of color is "representation." It is a burden one must discard as quickly as one begins to write. In front of the blank page, armed with research, a burning plot, and a story world that is alive in the writer's imagination, the number one responsibility of the writer must be to tell a good story. To my mind, it is hard to speak for a nation of more than 200 million people. Don't try. However, the writer does have a responsibility to be *respectful*.

I created a reading group of fellow Nigerians both at home and in the diaspora. My requirement of them was for "cultural sensitivity." They were my litmus test for the question: did my characters come across as authentic and reflect the contemporary lived experiences of fellow Nigerians?

I also visited the town where the real crime took place. I interviewed locals and asked for their version of events and why they thought something like this could have happened in their community. I wasn't seeking to "represent" anyone, but I wanted to find common threads in their version of events. Did they have any premonition of the tragedy? What was the prevalent mindset at the time? How did the event change the town and how they perceived the world? How did they think the outside world perceived them? What could have been done differently? And most importantly, how could they ensure that such a thing never happened again?

Asking these questions and more is what I mean by *respecting* the source.

It wasn't all smooth sailing. I did crash and almost burn a number of times, especially when what I was discovering via research overwhelmed me. The stark fact that people could do this to other people kept me awake at night. That the numerous culprits in the real-life case had been whittled down to a few scapegoats irked me. This was my personal issue with the real-life case, and it drove my fiction. It inspired the actions of my main character. The lack of political willpower to enact policies and laws that curtail or eradicate "jungle justice" fueled my motivation to write. If I was lucky to get published, I hoped the story would contribute to the national discourse around extrajudicial justice in Nigeria.

I finished the book in a fever of sorts. I remember feeling accomplished. Not because I had written a great story, but because I felt I had presented my world in a manner that was compelling, rich, and textured. I had convincingly provided context, which I hoped would guide the reader toward a deeper understanding of my story world and, by extension, Nigeria. I was proud that I had accomplished what I consciously put into practice, with a clear intention and an unwavering eye on the desired outcome.

I graduated with a distinction and even won an award for my manuscript. The paperback edition of my novel made *The Times* (UK) bestseller list, climbing to No. 2. This was a validation of sorts. There is indeed a way to tell a story from my part of the world that offers context while delivering the entertainment requirement of crime fiction.

8.

As I began writing the sequel to *Lightseekers*, I would occasionally remember that prepublication review and freeze. I would second-guess myself, wondering if I was presenting the "sociological" landscape of my country rather than telling a story in a simple, easy-to-understand manner. I would ask myself if the story was entertaining enough, as racy and action-packed as readers expect from crime fiction. I would go for days without writing a word, despairing that this second book would be much worse than the first.

Then, I would remind myself of my chosen purpose as a crime writer: to present the humanity of my world and my country to the reader. To hold their attention and offer them a perspective of compassion and respect that they won't get from cable news. To show how we came to be here and, hopefully, invite an appreciation for a different kind of crime writing that delivers on entertainment *and* context.

It is this sweet spot that I have chosen to dedicate my writing life to finding.

## Reading Suggestions

Shawn Coyne, *The Story Grid: What Good Editors Know*

William Zinsser, *On Writing Well: The Classic Guide to Writing Nonfiction*

Albert Rutherford, *The Systems Thinker*

Draper L. Kauffman and Morgan D. Kauffman, *Systems 1: An Introduction to Systems Thinking*, 4th edition

Lajos Egri, *The Art of Creative Writing*

John Truby, *The Anatomy of Story*

Jane K. Cleland, *Mastering Suspense, Structure, and Plot*

Stephen King, *On Writing*

D.B.C. Pierre, *Release the Bats*

A. Trevor Thrall, *The 12 Week Year for Writers*

# On Violence

*Nadifa Mohamed in conversation with Leila Aboulela*

**Writers can be placed in certain categories—the pas-**
toral, the avant-garde, or the philosophical—based on the content
and style of their work. Other classifications, such as African, Muslim, and immigrant, are broader, and often don't take into account
the specificities of the writer's work. Leila Aboulela is a writer who
lives in Britain but whose background is far from what's considered
the British "norm." Her seven novels cover vast geographical and
emotional distances. We met virtually to discuss what it means to
write about subjects such as violence and to carve out a space for
our own imaginations and fascinations in the literary world. With
laughter and many diversions, we discussed the painful aspects of
writing as women from places seemingly beyond the Western
imagination, how the challenges of writing and publishing are
heightened by the misreading of our work, the microaggressions
we experience at public events, and the expectation that we will
represent a whole country or faith group in our books. It is rare to
be able to speak so openly with another writer who just "gets" it
and, as two writers who did not go through creative writing pro-

grams, we have had to work through these issues in a solitary and piecemeal way.

The proliferation of degrees and short courses in creative writing over the past decade has overlapped with an ebb and flow of interest in "immigrant" or "international" or "African" fiction, but there has been very little absorption of non-Western narratives into what students learn; the reading lists are still stubbornly homogeneous and fixed on a Western "canon." This can mean that writers from non-Western backgrounds are left unprepared about how they fit into the literary landscape and the particularities of what they will face. Has Martin Amis ever been told that he has been selected for a prize because he is "exotic"? Have book festivals ever said that more than three white women writers would be too many? Does Sally Rooney ever need to explain why she writes about the lives of university students rather than Irish politics? I'm guessing it's a "no" to all of these rhetorical questions, but for me and Leila and many other writers, these provocations have been part of our writing lives. In our conversation Leila quotes Yvonne Vera. Let me bring in here the inimitable Zora Neale Hurston, who wrote in her short story "Sweat," published in 1926, that life (and to me, writing) can be "Sweat, sweat, sweat! Work and sweat, cry and sweat, pray and sweat!" But in that labor is also our own liberation.

**Nadifa Mohamed:** So, Leila, when I invited you to take part in this conversation, you were excited, and one of the things you said was that you had been watching *The Godfather*, which had made you think about issues of representation and being a minority. Can you tell us more about your thoughts on *The Godfather* and your own work?

**Leila Aboulela:** *The Godfather* is about crime and family, but it is also about immigration. As the story moves through generations, we see how the family members become less Italian and more and more American. The novel (and films) were criticized for their portrayal of Italian-Americans as inherently violent, since in reality very few of them were involved in criminal activity. Apparently, the mafia never even used the term "Godfather," but this was another myth which appealed to the public.

**NM:** Fairly or unfairly, I think of *The Godfather* as a story about the excitement of power, politics, and violence and of people doing things that normal society doesn't allow; it's a kind of titillation. Do you think that that same kind of titillation is used in Britain when talking about the "other," whether that is a Muslim other or Black other?

**LA:** Yes, I think so, definitely. The author of *The Godfather*, Mario Puzo, said that the head of his family was his mother, who brought up seven children alone, and her stories of life in Sicily inspired his writing. In the book, though, she is represented by the patriarch, the "Godfather." There is obviously a market for works that see the "other" as violent but ultimately redeemable. Mario Puzo wanted a wide readership, and he succeeded in producing a bestseller.

America is based on immigration, but in Britain, Muslims are seen through the lens of the Empire. Colonial attitudes and prejudices still persist. Black and Muslim immigrants are outsiders expected to be grateful and to "know their place." They have to jump through hoops in order to belong; they have to prove themselves worthy by distancing themselves from all that is not deemed to be British.

**NM:** Can we talk about your novel *Minaret*? Which was published after 9/11, right?

**LA:** It was conceived well before 9/11. I started to write it a year before 9/11, and it was published in 2005. After it was published, it was read as a post-9/11 novel, but the ingredients had been there before. The pressure in the world had been building well before the 9/11 attacks. This infused the novel.

**NM:** What were the ingredients?

**LA:** The hostility toward Islam and Muslims which started in Britain with the Salman Rushdie affair (the protests against his novel *The Satanic Verses* in 1988) and then the media's anti-Arab stance when Saddam Hussein invaded Kuwait in 1990 and during the First Gulf War. These events occurred when I first moved to Britain and, as a young woman wearing a hijab, in my early twenties, a student with one baby and then two, I felt the hostility keenly and struggled with it. The word *Islamophobia* didn't exist then, but I was living it. My move from Sudan to Britain felt like a "coming down in the world"— words I used in the first sentence of *Minaret*. But I was also keen, in the novel, to chronicle a personal journey toward faith. This idea of a young girl who was Westernized back in Sudan, then comes to London and becomes a practicing Muslim, is a reversal of what was expected. That, to me, was the important aspect of the novel as I was writing it, but many people read it primarily as a breakthrough into a London mosque community. It was as if they didn't know that such people existed! For the first time, they were reading about a particular community. Characters, a love story—it was all received as an insider's tale, "representative" of a particular group.

Many white readers have similar, rigid expectations—that a text will be representative, informative, accurate, relevant. It then leads them to generalize from a single piece of fiction. And ultimately narrows down what is published and who gets published. I think we shouldn't accept, without question, any specific line of interrogation generated by the West, or measuring tools used by the West, or pre-assumptions made by the West. It is easy for the writer of color to fall into such traps, generating the same tropes and not offering anything new. Also, putting all writers of color in one group is itself a white construct. Why should we all be one? Why should we all be the same? We are completely different.

**NM:** We come from different parts of the world. We have different histories. Did you feel that you were part of a literary community at that point?

**LA:** Not at first, when the writing felt deeply personal, an expression of my homesickness and culture shock. But slowly, over time, I developed a sense of identity as a writer. I first started writing after moving to Scotland, and I thought of myself as an immigrant writer. But ultimately my work came to be seen as part of international and African literature, rather than specifically British immigrant literature. Most of my readers, the ones that have stuck with me, novel after novel . . .

**NM:** (laughs) It isn't such a chore, I'm sure they're doing it because they love and enjoy your novels.

**LA:** (laughs) Thanks. These loyal readers increasingly seem to be from Africa, Dubai, Pakistan—or they themselves are part of the diaspora in the West.

**NM:** You have reminded me about Abdulrazak Gurnah, who was awarded the Nobel Prize for Literature in 2021. He is a Tanzanian, Zanzibari, British writer and it was interesting to see who claimed ownership of him. The British sort of did, but he was mostly unknown, not the typical person to represent Britain on the world stage. Then the Zanzibaris and Tanzanians seemed to say, "Oh, yes, fantastic," but they didn't really know his work either. In Zanzibar, there's also the fact that he reads as Arab though to me he is Black, East African. So I saw Omani Arabs taking possession of him as well. Do you have that same conflict, where you feel as if you're pulled and tugged between different camps?

**LA:** Because the majority of Sudanese writers write in Arabic and I write in English, I often feel left out, even though the context of my work is closely tied to Sudan. I put in tremendous effort to make my books available in Sudan, to get them translated into Arabic and published locally. When I visit I am always welcomed with large events and media coverage—but I am of course an outsider, and I might not consistently meet the expectations of the Sudanese reader in terms of subject matter. I am more confident writing about the Sudan I know and grew up in (Khartoum in the 1970s and 1980s) or a historical Sudan (from research) than contemporary issues. Now that I live in Scotland and I have won two Scottish prizes, I'm considered a Scottish writer, and this is gratifying because it does matter to a writer to be appreciated closer to home. Prizes do play a big role in giving a writer an identity. When I won the Caine Prize, I was celebrated as an African writer even though in some circles Sudan wasn't considered African enough (and I was born in Egypt, which was even more problematic because academia has traditionally differentiated between North Africa and sub-Saharan Africa). I can see that in my own situation, winning Scottish and African prizes gave me a sense of belonging.

**NM:** Are you considered or do you consider yourself a Black writer?

**LA:** I tend not to describe the physical characteristics of my characters, but they are Black in a visceral sense, and readers respond to that. Growing up in North Sudan, I considered myself Arab rather than Black, but then, coming to Britain, I started to identify as Black both politically and ethnically—though I would not deny my Arab identity. I saw myself in Buchi Emecheta's work and in the novels of Abdulrazak Gurnah. Again, it's the strong connection with the Black African immigration experience. Arab immigration tends to be a different experience, and a lot of Arabs consider themselves to be white (physically, not culturally) even though they are not perceived as such. Then again, within Arab culture, Sudan and Somalia are very much marginalized.

**NM:** What was your relationship to violence within *Minaret*?

**LA:** I went into my imagination to write a scene in *Minaret* in which the woman is abused on a bus. It was only afterward that cases of Islamophobia began to be documented and that documentation was made accessible. The reality is even worse than what I wrote about in my novel.

**NM:** I don't know if this is your worry, but my worry is there's something problematic about the Muslim female body being used as a site of violence. You know, a body that you're meant to be saving, or that you are eroticizing as something very exotic and alluring, or as a foreign body in a niqab or abaya that's on your streets and shouldn't be there. How do you navigate your own writing of the female Muslim body?

**LA:** I try not to think too much about the reader. These things that you're saying, of course, they're true and they're there, but I must somehow pretend that they're not, because otherwise I would be always looking over my shoulder. I would be either justifying or challenging, and my biggest aim is for my writing to be unselfconscious, organic, the kind of writing that needs no validation from others. There's no end to readers' and critics' prejudices; the goalposts are always changing. You can never say the right thing all the time or please all the right people. It's an impossibility. There are other things that I consider more important. Who is the audience, for example? I think of the audience as the people I'm writing about, even though in terms of numbers, most likely the majority of the people who are going to buy the book are not the people I'm writing about. But it's important to me, from an ethical point of view, to assume that the community I'm writing about is going to read it, and therefore I must ask, what will they think of it? Would they be happy to read it? I'm writing for and from within the community. My intention is, as H. L. Mencken said, to "afflict the comfortable and comfort the afflicted." At the end of the day, I want the Muslim woman I am writing about to be comfortable with what I'm saying.

**NM:** I remember being asked in a virtual talk with a group in Minnesota if my novel *The Orchard of Lost Souls* was halal. I didn't know how to answer that; I think in the end I said, "It's as halal as real life." How can you comfort people if you also want to be truthful? That conflict is one that comes up again and again because often Somalis don't like it if I write about something upsetting or something ugly. Where are your boundaries in both providing comfort to the afflicted but also telling things in an unvarnished way?

**LA:** You have to be truthful; you have to say things in an unvarnished way. I think readers will feel affirmed if you're still upholding their values. I believe whatever horrors I read about Muslims, and I will engage with that difficult reality, however uncomfortable it makes me, but I won't engage with disrespect or contempt for my religion. There are so many horrific things that Muslims inflict on each other. Let's talk about FGM [female genital mutilation]. If somebody is writing from a purely Western point of view, then it is cast as violent, criminal, unacceptable, but when we are writing about it from our point of view, we also know that these women are our mothers and our grandmothers. They have inflicted violence on their daughters, but they have also shown tenderness and love. They're still looking after their children, struggling and sacrificing, and all this needs to be there in the story, while acknowledging that as progressives we want to stop this practice. We can't make monsters out of these women. We have to get inside their heads. We have to understand why they do this, and at the same time, we have to object to the practice.

**NM:** That raises the specter of cultural relativity, which I think of as something that's very maligned at the moment. The idea that different cultures can respond to different acts in different ways. So in a Somali context, a mother who is organizing FGM for her daughters does not see it as an act of violence at all; it's seen as a rite of passage, it's seen as a moment of celebration. When an act is not even understood as violence, and you're trying to be true to those characters and that cultural milieu, is the writer still obligated to see it as violence?

**LA:** Well, yes, because from the point of view of the child it *is* violence. She still feels the pain, she still goes through the agony, and if something goes wrong then she's stuck with a medical problem. There are repercussions that we need to write about, and people do write about that all over the Muslim world. It's the making a monster out of the mother that we should be careful not to do as writers from this heritage.

**NM:** I feel that if there is any complexity in discussing a subject like FGM, the Western reader might balk at it, because it is seen in such a linear way—this is bad, the people that do it are bad, they're not good parents, and the children need to be taken away from them. The Western reader can demand things. I think they can also impose a moral framework that doesn't fit neatly onto other worlds.

**LA:** That's true, but at the end of the day, as the late Yvonne Vera told me, the writer leads the reader. Writing a novel is about putting oneself in a leadership role, with the reader following, not the other way around. If the reader wants to come along for the ride, well and good. If they are uncomfortable and want to turn away, they can turn away. Also, in ten or twenty years, who knows what the reader is going to balk at or accept? What the Western reader demands changes over time, as does what we even mean when we say "Western" reader.

There's another elephant in the room, which is the size of the readership. Publishers want as many people as possible to read their books, but this can adversely affect what gets published and what gets written. To make a book appealing to as many readers as possible, you have to make it less culturally challenging.

**NM:** Homogenized?

**LA:** Yes. The bigger the platform, the more toned down and palatable the material needs to be.

**NM:** Do you think that the successful novels by nonwhite writers are homogenized in some way?

**LA:** Not the ones I read. Serious writers, those with integrity, are always pushing the boundaries. They can mix the familiar with the new to appeal to more readers while at the same time challenging them. There's also the demographic factor. More people of color are buying books. Who, as a newly arrived immigrant or refugee, is going to buy a hardback novel for fourteen pounds? But in time their children will. On Instagram, today's young immigrant women are posting, "Oh, here is my book haul"; I doubt their mothers were buying that many books. I feel this change too in other parts of the world. You go to festivals in Lahore or Lagos, and there are all these young people buying books like they're buying snacks. It's just wonderful.

**NM:** That speaks to a class difference as well between the parents and child, which also changes the way they want to hear stories. I think the older generation was restrictive about what they wanted their children to learn. That could be because they thought that, if they were too open, the children would become too Westernized, or it could be the result of trauma that they're holding and protecting their children from.

**LA:** What is also true is that certain books are published at the right time, when readers want something a little bit edgy, a little bit different. I was living in Scotland when *Trainspotting* came out, and I witnessed its explosive success. This is an interesting example for another reason: although the novel contained such a negative depiction of a particular community,

Irvine Welsh was not burdened with having to worry about representing Scotland to the world.

**NM:** Maybe not Scotland, but his characters are rarely seen in popular culture or arts. So his portrayal becomes *the* portrayal and therefore likely to be criticized if he's inaccurate in any way.

**LA:** Yes, but in his case, people are aware that he is writing about a specific community. They understand the context. But with us, it doesn't happen. That's why we have this anxiety, that's why we're having this conversation, because we're dealing with a readership and a publishing industry that doesn't fully understand the nuances or context of our material. We have to care about accuracy because the text is going to pass through editors and subeditors and copy editors who may not have a clue about the background. In terms of a reader assuming that this is what Somalia or Sudan is based on a single novel, we can't control that; the onus is on them not to make this assumption.

**NM:** What have been the most memorable misconceptions of Sudan that you've heard in events or from interviewers?

**LA:** That everyone is poor. That no middle class or upper class exists. Early in my career I went to Germany; I was speaking to an audience about *The Translator,* and a German woman stood up. She shouted, "I don't want to hear about educated Sudanese who can afford to travel to the West. People are starving in your country and you should write about that."

She was upset, and she does have a point, but the solution isn't that I write about refugee camps, which I have no clue about. The solution is that she should read other Sudanese writers who have focused on these subjects.

**NM:** It's also very hubristic on her part because she's not only saying that you should be writing about something else, but she's also saying that your own experience or even your existence is uninteresting to her. That's quite dangerous.

**LA:** Yes, it is. But if she's making these choices in a marketplace where there's a lot of availability, then she can, as a reader, make this particular choice and say, "Well, you know, I would rather read about a person in a refugee camp than read about somebody who can afford to travel." That's her choice.

**NM:** I've been working as a published writer for years, but I'm only now realizing how degrading and traumatic those reader interactions can be. I did a virtual event in Scotland recently, and an older man got up and said, "I hear you talking badly about Britain and talking about the justice system and all of these things, and I want to know, why do you stay in this country if you dislike it so much?" I've had that question before, and I came down hard on him immediately, but I find that transition from writing being a private activity to a public one challenging. When you write, you feel like no one is watching, no one is listening, and then, when you present your work to the outside world, race, politics, expectations, and everything else come very hard at you. How have you navigated that?

**LA:** It was harder, I think, at the time of that German incident, which was in 2002, a year after September 11. Those years were pretty rough. At events, people would ask "Why do you dress like that?" There were attempts to "divide and rule" writers from Muslim backgrounds, into groups such as liberal, moderate, secular, or conservative. People commenting, as I signed their books, "Why aren't you dressed like the other (non-hijab-wearing) writer on the panel?" Now, it's quieting down, and I don't get a lot of these responses.

**NM:** You said something very interesting just now about a sense of divide and rule between you and secular Muslim authors. You write about sex and other things that a conservative Muslim would not want to read about. So it's not as if you are holding a strict line about what you represent and don't represent in your work. I wouldn't think of it as being different to the writings of secular Muslims, whatever that means.

**LA:** The difference is that I write about Islam as a valid faith affecting the characters' actions and perspectives, rather than a culture or tradition.

**NM:** You're not apologetic about it?

**LA:** I center it, and I don't take into account what the readership is going to think. There's this line, for example, in *Minaret* where the main character fantasizes about becoming a concubine. It comes in this context: "I stare down at my hands, my warped self and distorted desires. I would like to be his family's concubine, like something out of *The Arabian Nights*, with life-long security and a sense of belonging. But I must settle for freedom in this modern time."

**NM:** I remember that line.

**LA:** Despite the context, the character's self-awareness that this is "distorted," as well as the irony, critics reprimanded me for this line time and time again. So, in my new novel, set in nineteenth-century Sudan, which I just sent to the publisher, a concubine is the main character. My attitude is, "You can't swallow concubines. Good. There you go. Good."

**NM:** The history of slavery is also rarely seen in Muslim literature. So even that reference to concubines in *Minaret* startled me because it's hidden in most fiction.

**LA:** People are ashamed of the slave trade on the east coast of Africa.

**NM:** Somalia was a slave-trading country. Sudan, parts of Ethiopia, the whole of Zanzibar, but it just seems to have been completely erased from the public imagination.

**LA:** It is hidden because of shame, but also because the enslaved were eventually fully integrated into the families. They became somebody's mum or grandmother, and nobody wants to be told that your grandmother was a concubine. In these very patriarchal societies it almost doesn't matter who the mother is. You are your father's child, so you are legally born free with all the rights of the other children. Then the mother piggybacks on the child, attains manumission, and her status rises in the community. That is different from slav-

ery in the West, where it didn't matter that you are the master's child; you are still a slave because your mother is a slave,
and, of course, because you're Black. Reading and writing
about the past, and being immersed in landscapes that are
pre-modern, can almost feel like science fiction, like having to
inhabit a different world. Incidentally, once at an event, an elderly white man said that reading my work was like reading
science fiction. I thought that was bizarre, but an interesting
way of engaging with texts from completely different cultures.

**NM:** You agree with him?

**LA:** To some extent, because the reader is entering a world
where the rules are different, the parameters are different or
even inimical. This is preferable to being judged by Western
maxims. I didn't know that cultural relativity is a bad thing. As
writers of color, it is not only our identity or minority experience which can shape our work. It's how we view the world
using our rich heritage and non-Western perspectives. This is
how we can add something new to English literature.

*Reading Suggestions from Nadifa Mohamed*

Toni Morrison, *Playing in the Dark: Whiteness and the
    Literary Imagination*
Arundhati Roy, *Azadi*
Shani Mootoo, *Cereus Blooms at Night*
Rohinton Mistry, *A Fine Balance*
Kamel Daoud, *The Meursault Investigation*

## Reading Suggestions from Leila Aboulela

Tayeb Salih, *Season of Migration to the North*

Shashi Deshpande, *The Dark Holds No Terror*

Buchi Emecheta, *Second-Class Citizen*

Abdulrazak Gurnah, *Gravel Heart*

Ahdaf Soueif, *In the Eye of the Sun*

Frantz Fanon, *Black Skin, White Masks*

Edward Said, *Culture and Imperialism*

# On Art and Activism

*Myriam Gurba*

## UNO: ADORO A MIS MUERTITOS

**I'm the granddaughter of two "unknown" Mexican** artists.

Quotation marks frame the word because it begs the question, *unknown to whom?* These artists aren't unknown to me. These artists raised and shaped me, making me an artist. My primary art form is writing. My secondary art form is living. These two practices beget one another.

En nuestra familia, we write to paint ourselves into eternity.

En nuestra familia, we paint to write ourselves into eternity.

It doesn't always go as planned.

My grandfather Ricardo had a sense of humor about his literary failures. He bragged that he was a man of "puro cuento," a bard, and he loved to talk to anyone who'd listen about his unpublished novels—all six of them. These page-turners were destined not only to make him a household name; they would ensure his immortality, too. His imagination was a library brimming with classics written by him, and I've never seen a man delight more in his own words than my grandfather. The narcissistic web that he spun for ninety-seven years was, perhaps, his most dazzling masterpiece.

My grandfather also wrote poetry, and he inflicted his sappy cantos and sonnets on anyone who couldn't escape. He boasted that his literary friends, Arturo Rivas Sáinz, Adalberto Navarro Sánchez, and Juan José Arreola, once nominated him as their poet laureate, presenting him with a signed certificate that gave him this status. I've never seen this alleged credential, and while I have doubts about its existence, I want this legend to be true.

My grandfather had an exquisite talent for building verbal monuments to himself.

My grandmother, Arcelia, was his opposite. She's the grandparent I spent more time with.

Whereas my grandfather instrumentalized art, exploiting it as a tool of self-promotion, my grandmother quietly made art with people, her creative expression forging social and spiritual bonds. Art was how she connected with, and cared for, my mother, father, brother, sister, and me. She painted portraits of us, but the paintings never seemed solely hers. The portraits were *ours*, creations by both painter and subject. These works were collaborations, dialogues, and, at times, battles of the will. It was challenging to sit for my grandmother when I was a child. Sometimes, to keep me from fidgeting, I required a bribe.

In the portraits my grandmother painted of me, I can see her eye, her art teacher's eye, my parents, and my stubborn spirit. Brushstrokes unified us, and through art, my grandmother taught me less about empathy and more about the magic of interdependence.

I learned that art requires love. Like activism, art is a warm and caring thing to be done with others. The notion that art is performed alone is illusory, a strange and damaging lie.

My grandmother's and grandfather's spirits have left their bodies, but I tightly cling to their lessons. My grandfather's is cautionary: Speak loudly and create a spectacle but don't fall too in love with your own words. My grandmother's lesson is communitarian: Art makes society. It enlivens community just as community enlivens it. My grandmother modeled a profoundly "un-American" approach to life, society, and artmaking, demonstrating that art should be made for the sake of the collective, never arte por el arte.

Each day, I put to use the lessons given to me by mis muertitos, my beloved dead.

## DOS: NOS LLAMABAMOS LAS GUAYABAS

During the aughts, a desire to be in community with like-minded women led me to a circle of Latina writers, Las Guayabas.

Guayabas (in English the word sounds ugly and harsh: *guavas*) are a tropical fruit native to México. I prefer the sexy, pink variety instead of the white kind, and a cheerful guayabo grew in the front yard of my small, blue house in Long Beach, California, the unofficial headquarters of Las Guayabas. Members included tatiana de la tierra, Carriben Fragoza, Estella Gonzales, and Griselda Suarez. Except for one Guayaba, we were all Chicanas, U.S.-born women of Mexican ancestry.

tatiana was born in Villavicencio, Colombia. She and I share a birthday, May 14, and as our collective's eldest, tatiana was our most seasoned activist and writer. She was also our brashest member. Her best friend, Olga, told me that when the two of them met in graduate school, nuestra Colombiana reached for a handshake as she proclaimed, "Hi, I'm tatiana de la tierra, and I write cunt stories." tatiana voiced her pussy prose in Spanglish, Spanish, and English, and in the '90s, she'd teamed up with three other women to publish the first international Latina lesbian magazine, *esto no tiene nombre*. Between its glossy covers, readers could find everything from old-fashioned advice columns to pornography starring tatiana.

Guayabas are a soft fruit, and like them, our collective remained malleable, becoming what we needed it to be. That's how collectives and mutual aid societies are supposed to work. You give what you can, when you can, how you can, and you take only what you need. Las Guayabas were leaderless, but that didn't make us aimless. We gave others and ourselves what we needed when we needed it, giving what we could where we could. Sometimes, what we needed was to talk and be heard, and on Saturday afternoons, we convened in my living room to speak. My house rabbits would hop about, listening to us with their long floppy ears. We shared information about publishing, literary craft, employment, and sociopolitical organizing. We also shared good old chisme. Our get-togethers were like very loose, consciousness-raising circles. They also felt rather like Spanglish coven meetings.

Las Guayabas shared our writing, both aloud and on the page. Doing so among Latinas was important to me. Because of our ethnic and ancestral affinities, we didn't have to do the added racialized labor that many of us were tired of. If you're a minoritized writer, you likely know what I'm referring to. In writing workshops where whiteness dominates, too many of us are told that our work is "exotic" and therefore "unmarketable." We're advised to make the work more palatable to white taste buds. Some white audiences further pressure minoritized writers to act as cultural ambassadors, treating us as tour guides and reducing our homes and communities to vacation destinations for the white imagination.

In my living room, these pressures didn't exist. Having been raised similarly, Las Guayabas understood one another. While our backgrounds weren't identical, there was enough in common to bridge certain differences. We could have luxurious conversations about metaphor, metonym, and motive without being derailed by questions such as, "Is there electricity in Mexico?"

Las Guayabas hosted readings and writing workshops. In 2009, we spoke as a panel at the Los Angeles Latino Book and Family Festival, discussing the use of profanity in our work. We opened our presentation by inviting audience members to share their favorite curse words. It's always exciting to hear girls and women from minoritized communities share the profane words that they hold dearest, and it's even more exciting to hear the rationale behind our chosen favorites. In that shared festival space, which became paradoxically sacred, we could be honest about our relationships with words and art. Such safety is so precious.

## Tres: Pendejada

My grandparents and parents raised me to understand that since its inception, the United States of America has exploited and abused Latin America. In 2019, a novel that operates as part of this ongoing exploitative project made its way into my lap.

An editor at a feminist magazine invited me to review Jeanine Cummins's *American Dirt*. I hadn't heard of the book or its author, but based on its title, I assumed that it told a soil-based story, a farmer's fable. Oddly, the authors who'd blurbed it weren't experts in pedology. Horror, mystery, and crime writers, including heavy hitters Stephen King and Don Winslow, hailed _American Dirt_ as a must-read, likening it to John Steinbeck's _The Grapes of Wrath_.

Several months earlier, I'd reviewed Cherrie Moraga's _Native Country of the Heart_ for this same feminist magazine. Moraga is Mexican American, and I imagine I was tasked with reviewing her work because of our similar heritage. I found it exciting that an editor had now asked me to review a book on dirt. The invitation suggested that I wasn't being ethnically pigeonholed. I wasn't a one-trick pony, my sole trick being my Mexican-ness. My editor believed I had range.

Later, while visiting family in México, I discovered that my Mexicanness was, indeed, what my editor was after. I was disappointed, and I read _American Dirt_ during November in Guadalajara. The book turned out to be a narco-thriller, a clumsy wannabe Mexican Franken-tale that crudely stitches together every noxious Mexican trope.

According to the moral universe of _American Dirt_, a cesspool of amoral violence begins at the U.S.-Mexico border, presumably stretching all the way to Patagonia. The United States, John Winthrop's proverbial "city on a hill," is the novel's North Star, its beacon. Only in the U.S. will migrants enjoy prosperity, abundance, democracy, and the rule of law. The plot of _American Dirt_ evokes pity for migrants, who all seem to be running from machete-wielding psychopaths instead of crises triggered by U.S. foreign policy and rampant global misogyny.

After finishing _American Dirt_, I decided to use one of my favorite forms of activism: gossip. Activism need not be a pyrotechnic on-slaught, a spectacularly public fight manifested through picketing, marching, or dicey face-to-face confrontations with authority. For women and girls, activism has historically involved subtle attacks and acts of sabotage. Gossip provides a great instrument for this type of warfare. By whispering chisme to carefully chosen listeners, we send news to the four cardinal directions. The best listeners are those who will compulsively share what we tell them.

Gossip, when it truthfully exposes shitty deeds, warns, shames, and protects. It's also easily transmitted through the internet. Femi-nist scholar Paula Ray has written that social networking sites are "quickly becoming a means of facilitating gender-based activism." She also notes that his method is compatible with women's tradi-tional domestic duties, allowing us to partake in activism "from the confines of [our kitchens.]"

Gossip can also take the form of a book review, and I used mine to warn audiences about the narco-thriller masquerading as a work of social realism. After emailing my review to my editor, I thought I could roll my sleeves back down and get to work on other projects. I was wrong. Too much money had been invested in *American Dirt*. It was poised to be a bestseller.

My editor rejected my review. Her decision to suppress it led me to self-publish it through social media. This gonzo gesture reached a large audience; I had clearly learned from my grandfather how to get audiences to listen to me. Though he failed to achieve notoriety as a poet and novelist, he succeeded at becoming a much sought-after publicist. Part of a publicist's job is to whisper the right stories into the right ears and hope that they stir interest. The review did that, and one reader privately contacted me to gossip, sharing what was then still a secret: *American Dirt* was shielded from flopping because it had been blessed by Oprah Winfrey.

The narco-thriller would be receiving her book club's imprimatur.

After learning this secret, the monstrous marketing campaign promoting *American Dirt* finally made sense. Its shitty stereotypes and white-savior-ism were going to be devoured by millions of white liberals who would pat themselves on the back for learning about "the brown masses." My critique of the narco-thriller's intended audience was inspired by the integrity modeled by my grandmother. We don't make art for art's sake. We make it for people's sake, and precisely because *American Dirt* opposes our collective interests, I wanted to struggle with other Latines to oppose it.

I considered writing an essay that would critique the publishing industry's white supremacy and misogyny. I knew that could result in fewer professional writing opportunities, but I didn't care. I figured that if opportunities dried up because of my critique, I could continue to release my written work estilo rasquache. Rasquachismo is a Chicane style of DIY art-making and self-publishing that relies on repurposing conventional objects. For example, a rasquache book might look like a zine printed on recycled paper, the paper stitched to covers hewn of scavenged cardboard.

With a commitment to rasquachismo in mind, I wrote the essay. In it, I also discussed the rejection of my review by the feminist magazine. An academic blog, *Tropics of Meta*, published the essay, and it went viral. Like many female activists, I received hate mail and threats. I also received messages of support and invitations to collaborate with other activists. One of these invitations came from

Roberto Lovato, a San Francisco–based writer of El Salvadoran ancestry. Lovato asked me if I wanted to participate in more actions against *American Dirt*, and he explained that he'd been involved in a campaign to oust anti-Latine bigot Lou Dobbs, who used CNN as a bully pulpit to espouse xenophobic rhetoric.

I enthusiastically agreed to work with him.

Although *American Dirt* made the bestseller list, the imprint responsible for it, Flatiron Books, went to war against us. The imprint issued a press release suggesting that angry and uncontrollable Latines were stirring up resentment that could lead to violence against Cummins. Soon thereafter, celebrity authors, like Stephen King, tweeted that writers should not have to fear for their lives. These responses drew even more attention to *American Dirt*. Interviewers asked me if I thought my viral essay had played a part in boosting the book's sales and I answered, "No." I explained that the publishing industry has a machine in place that creates bestsellers, Oprah Winfrey's Book Club imprimatur being a vital part of that machine.

Along with Lovato, writer David Bowles, and activists working for the organization Presente, we launched an art-and-town-hall initiative. We created activist tool kits for participants. We called our initiative Dignidad Literaria and urged writers and artists to host town hall meetings. These provided space to discuss white supremacy in the arts and literature, representation in publishing, and what collective steps we ought to take next. We also gave tips for curating art happenings that would center the work of Latine writers. Passionate town hall discussions took place on both the West and East coasts. Art happenings did too. One of them was organized by poet Xochitl-Julisa Bermejo and was held at Vroman's, the Pasadena bookstore where Cummins's Los Angeles–area event had been canceled.

Publishing executives invited Lovato, Bowles, and me to discuss the burgeoning social movement incited by the resistance to *American Dirt*. We flew to New York and sat with these executives at a conference table. One lectured me about my tone, reprimanding me for being "mean" to his friend "Jeanine." This pissed me off. I wanted to respond that it was also pretty mean to publish and promote a racist, xenophobic, and misogynistic narco-thriller, one that our fascist president could use to further demonize migrants. The meeting was catered. A box of sandwiches sat in the middle of the table. I didn't touch them.

Our meeting yielded mixed results. Flatiron agreed to establish a diversity, equity, and inclusion committee. They also stated that they would hire Latine editors and publish more Latine titles. To their credit, Flatiron has released more titles written by Latine authors and diversified their staff. However, they're still pushing *American Dirt*, and I don't think that the kind of change I'd like to see can happen until racial capitalism dies. Until then, we engage in stopgap measures.

## CUATRO: COLLEAGUES AREN'T COMRADES

I was teaching high school social studies as the *American Dirt* saga was unfolding, and my students paid careful attention to the literary activism its publication provoked.

Some of the kids decided to participate.

One afternoon, an excited pair of students chirped, "Ms. Gurba!

We saw that book that you wrote about on a table at Target. We took all the copies and hid them in the bathroom! Look!"

The student showed me a picture of her sister scooping books off a table. She showed me another of her sister hiding the books.

I laughed.

Other students who'd read the viral essay visited me to discuss it. They agreed with its analysis and sentiments. I was working at a "minority majority" school whose student body was predominantly Latine, and many of the kids felt that they had a personal stake in the fight against *American Dirt*. One student told me that my essay was being discussed in their literature class and said that their teacher had commented that I was a "surprisingly good" writer.

"What do you think that teacher finds so surprising about my ability to write well?" I asked the student.

The kid, a Mexican American, laughed.

We both knew what was implied by their teacher's statement.

I was told by another student that his writing teacher had said that I was a shitty critic, that I didn't understand "the purpose of fiction." He told the student that fiction is a place where anything can happen and that my criticism of the narco-thriller's inauthenticity failed to recognize that.

I told the student, "Yeah, fiction is a place where anything can happen, but *American Dirt* is being marketed as social *realism*. My condemnation of the book came from the likelihood that white liberal readers were going to pick up *American Dirt*, a work of fiction, and consume it as fact. I laid out that argument in my essay which I don't think your teacher actually read. Most people who are butt-hurt about the essay haven't read it."

The student agreed and told me that that same teacher had made resentful remarks about having Central American migrants in his class. My blood began to boil.

I felt like Chicana non grata on campus. Faculty and administrators who had previously treated me with civility or indifference were chilly or hostile. I figured that some were acting that way because they felt "attacked" by my essay. They were those white liberal readers whom *American Dirt* was written for, and they wanted a pat on the back for reading about migrants.

One afternoon, two kids working on the school newspaper came to interview me, and the next issue of the paper featured me on the cover. The headline announced, "Poly Teacher Calls Out 'Pendeja' and Sparks Social Movement." The article endorsed my critique. The day after I made the cover, two administrators, two security guards, and an armed police officer came to my classroom. One of the administrators told me to surrender my keys and leave campus immediately. When I asked her why, she answered that my social media use was disruptive to the learning environment. I asked her to show me an official document confirming her statement. She said that she had none and that I needed to follow her. Given the timing of my eviction from my classroom, I believe that my critique of *American Dirt*, and my critique of the school district's atrocious response to the students' accusations, were among the driving forces behind my placement on administrative leave. As students watched, the cohort marched me off campus in a shameful and frightening manner. I began to cry out of rage and frustration. As I wept, the policewoman removed her phone, aimed it at me, and took pictures, impromptu mugshots. She spun around and marched away, followed by the security guards. Before the administrators left, they told me that I was prohibited from discussing what had just happened.

I immediately took to Twitter and described exactly what had just happened.

My students were assigned a substitute teacher who told them that they were banned from speaking about me. The new teacher even told the kids that they were not allowed to say "Gurba."

*How ridiculous,* I thought. *They just incentivized the kids to chant my name. A lot.*

And they did. Soon after, a group of students led a direct action, holding a rally in protest of my banishment and attempted silencing. They carried signs and chanted, and one student messaged me a photograph of the demonstration.

"Ms. Gurba," she wrote, "this is all for you."

I cried when I saw the photos.

The kids had listened, watched, and taken notes during the struggle against that stupid little book. They had learned a lot.

## CINCO: ESCRITURA Y CRIATURA

We speak, paint, write, and otherwise struggle our way into existence.

We give birth to ourselves over and over through these practices.

My activism and writing are inextricable, and by now, it should be clear how my activism guides my hand when I author nonfiction. When I write fiction, my politics also guides my hand as I attempt to commemorate communities, histories, and ecosystems that are either ignored or distorted by the bigoted gaze. When I write fiction, I borrow heavily from Mexican and Chicane folk traditions, centering folk figures, such as La Llorona, and folk practices, such as quinceañeras. The decision to use such tropes is literary, as these figures and practices animate plot and communicate theme, but they're also political gestures. Through my short stories, I fatten the canon of U.S. literature with Chicanisms and Mexicanisms.

I wrote much of my fiction, which was published in the collections *Dahlia Season* and *Painting Their Portraits in Winter,* while adhering to a strict writing schedule. I have worked as a high school teacher for most of my writing life, and because most campuses require a teacher to be in the classroom prior to eight o'clock, I wake at five in the morning and write as the dark sky welcomes the sun. I do this for an hour each weekday and dedicate my Saturdays and Sundays to more writing and artmaking. Writing is a form of medicine for me, and so I always find a way to do it, even during chaotic or challenging times. If need be, I'll go for walks and compose narrative between my ears.

There's always a way to write.

I often bring different types of humor to my writing. I started incorporating humor into my work after I realized that no matter how much gravitas a narrative has, there will be plenty of readers who refuse to take my work seriously due to my social position. Fuck them. Humor is a way of commiserating with the reader, especially when very culturally specific humor is in use, and this approach allows me to create a sense of cultural intimacy with audiences. By being funny on the page, I assert that humor is also a woman's weapon.

My ancestors give me the strength to continue devoting myself to various struggles. I appeal to their spirits for protection, vision, and guidance. In return, I protect and cherish their memory. I honor them regularly, making offerings of food and drink. I pray to them in the same way some people pray to Jesus. I was raised to think about death often, to understand that Death is everywhere, an entity who might enfold us in Her arms at any moment. This worldview isn't morbid. Instead, it's one that requires us to value life, to consider how precious it is. Death reminds me that someday, flowers might spring from my remains. I want to be sure that those flowers are the good kind, a necessary medicine for future generations.

## Reading Suggestions

Carribean Fragoza, *Eat the Mouth That Feeds You*
Estella González, *Chola Salvation*
tatiana de la tierra, *For the Hard Ones*

# On the Second Person

*Kiese Laymon*

*You know that any resemblance to real places, spaces,*
*people, time, or things is purely coincidental.*

**Alone, you sit on the floor of your apartment thinking** about evil, honesty, that malignant growth in your hip, your dead uncle, letters you should have written, the second person, and stretch marks. You're wearing an XXL T-shirt you plan on wearing the day your novel comes out. The front of the T-shirt says, WHAT'S A REAL BLACK WRITER? The back reads, FUCK YOU. PAY ME. You open your computer. With a scary pain in your hip, you inhale and force a crooked smile before reading an e-mail from Brandon Farley, your fifty-four-year-old Black editor.

The success of your book will be partially dependent on readers who have a different sensibility than your intended audience [*he writes*]. As I've already said to you, too many sections of the book feel forced for the purpose of discussing racial politics. Think social media. Think comment sections. Those white people buy books, too, bro. Readers, especially white readers, are tired of Black writers playing the wrong race card. If you're gonna play it (and I think you should) play it right. Look at Tarrantino [*sic*]. He is about to fool all these people into believing they were watching a Black movie with Django. I guarantee you that whiteness will anchor almost every scene. That's one model you should think about.

Also, Black men don't read. And if they did, they wouldn't read this kind of fiction. So you might think of targeting bougie Black women readers. Bougie Black women love plot. They love romance with predictable Boris Kodjoe–type characters. Or they love strong sisters caught up in professional hijinks who have no relationships with other sisters. Think about what holds a narrative like *Scandal* together.

In 2012, real Black writers make the racial, class, gender, and sexual politics of their work implicit. Very implicit. The age of the "race narrative" is over, bro. As is, the only way your book would move units is if Oprah picked it for her Book Club. That's not happening. Oprah only deals with real Black writers.

You begin typing.

Hey Brandon, this is my fourteenth thorough revision for you in four years. I know I'm not changing your mind and that's fine. Thanks for telling me what real Black writers do and what Oprah likes. You never told me you met her. Anyway, the Black teenagers in my book are actually pur-

posely discussing "racial politics" in awkwardly American
ways. Their race and racial politics, like their sexuality and
sexual politics, is somehow tied to every part of their character. My book is unapologetically an American race novel,
among other things. I'm still not sure why you bought the
book if you didn't dig the vision.

You push send on the e-mail before opening up the Word doc
you just defended. You jump to Chapter Nine. Thirty minutes later,
a section of the book where an older queer coach tries to impart a
strange "them versus us" racial understanding on your narrator is
cut because it "explicitly discusses racial politics."

You call your editor names that hurt, muddied misogynist
names you pride yourself on never calling any human being while
looking out the tall window of your second-floor apartment in
Poughkeepsie, New York.

A barefoot white boy with a red and black lumberjack shirt is
outside sitting under an oak tree. He's doing that walkie-talkie thing
on his phone that you fucking hate. You can tell he's telling the
truth and lying at the same time.

"*You* fucking hurt me more than anyone in my whole life," he
says. "I couldn't hate *you* . . . I just don't trust *you* . . . You're the second person who has done this to me. *You're* the one who said *you* tell
the truth . . . *You* started this." The white boy is scratching his sack
with his left thumb and using his big toe to make designs in the dirt
in front of him. "*You* ruined my life and hurt me way more than I
hurt *you*. It's always all about *you*."

You wonder about the second person on the other end of the

phone. Is the second person a woman or a man? Is s/he listening to the lumberjack on speakerphone? Is s/he wishing the lumberjack would hurry up and finish so s/he can run and get a two-for-one special on Peanut Buster Parfaits from Dairy Queen? You know far too well why a first or third person could self-righteously claim innocence in matters of love and loss, but you can't figure out why the lumberjack is scratching his sack with his thumb and making dirt rainbows with his big toe.

Looking down at the browning S key on your keyboard, you think more hateful thoughts about your editor, your ex-girlfriend, skinny people, and fat young Black men. These thoughts distract you from the pain in your hip, the dirt on your hands.

For five years, Brandon Farley, your editor, has had you waiting.

You remember the acidic sweetness in Grandma's voice when you told her you'd just signed a two-book deal with KenteKloth Books, the most popular African American imprint in the country. New York fall felt like Mississippi winter as Grandma came out of her second diabetic coma.

"We are so proud of you, baby," Grandma whispered over the phone from Forest, Mississippi. "Just remember that God gave you five senses and whatever health you got for a reason. When they gone, they gone, but if you don't use them best you can while you got them, ain't a bigger fool in the world than that fool in the mirror."

Six months before your first novel's initial publication date of June 2009, you stopped hearing from Brandon Farley. He didn't answer your calls or respond to e-mails. You gave up and called the publisher of KenteKloth in February.

"Oh, Brandon didn't tell you?" his boss, Ms. Jacoby, asked. "He's no longer with us, but your book has been picked up by Nathalie Bailey. She'll call you in a few days."

Your lungs whistled, crashed, and slipped into the heels of your feet. You told yourself it would be okay. Then trudged your sexy ass to the International House of Pancakes.

Three hours later, you were full, fatter than you wanted to be, less sexy than you were, and you found a way to reach Brandon Farley at home. Brandon apologized for not telling you he wasn't seeing eye-to-eye with his boss. He promised you that Nathalie Bailey was a friend of his who would do right by both your novels.

A week later you got a call from Nathalie. "It's a hard sell for Black literary fiction these days," she told you. "But I like what you're doing. You're on your way to becoming a real Black writer. It's a gorgeous book with big messy ideas, and we've got to work hard and fast. But I'd love for you to let me take this book to publication. It's a winner."

You felt a comfort with Nathalie, but you didn't want to be impulsive like you were with Brandon. "Can I have a few days to think about it?" you asked her. "Just to make sure."

A few days passed and you planned on calling Nathalie at 4:00 P.M. on a Thursday. At 3:00 P.M. you got a call from a 212 number. Before you had a book deal, 917 and 212 numbers were like slimming mirrors; they made you think, *Damn nigga, you ain't that disgusting at all.*

On the other end of 917 and 212 numbers were agents, editors, or an ex telling you she was sorry and she missed sharing a heartbeat.

"Hello," you answered, trying to sound busy and country at the same time.

"Hi."

It was Brandon Farley.

After a few minutes of spin where Brandon Farley showed you how much he remembered about your book and how happy he was to be the new senior editor of young adult fiction at the widely acclaimed Duck Duck Goose Publishing Company, he said, "All that to say, we really want your book."

"Word?"

"Word up, bro!" Brandon laughed. It was the first time any Black man on earth had ever called you "bro" with a long *o*.

"Bro," he said it again, "I will pay you more for one book than you got for two over at KenteKloth. I'll want an option of first refusal on the second. But that'll still give you the kind of flexibility you want."

"Are you serious?" you asked. "Only thing is, I'm a little worried about changing the subtext and the darkness and the metafictive stuff if it's gonna be marketed as a young adult book. The ending ain't really pretty."

"You'd be surprised at the possibilities in young adult fiction," he told you. "Listen, bro, young adults will read it. This is adult literary fiction with mass appeal. You won't have to make many changes at all, and we can get you a pub date of June 2009."

"But what about Nathalie?" you asked.

"Bro, you're the second person to ask me about her," he scoffed, sounding like a hungry hip-hop mogul. You hated even imagining using the word *scoffed*.

"It's business, bro. Never personal. You'll have to get out of that contract over there. And I've got the perfect agent for you. She's this wonderful fine sister over at Chatham Ward & Associates named

Bobbie Winslow. Look her up. Bobbie'll take care of everything if you decide to go with us."

You smiled and forgave him for four or five "bros" too many.

Later that day, Bobbie, the perfect agent/fine sister, called from a 212 number and asked you to send her the other pieces you were working on. By 8:00 P.M., you sent her the book Brandon wanted, another novel, and a rough draft of some essays you'd been working on. By 3:00 A.M., she e-mailed you and said, "We want you. You're the second person I've said this to in five years, but I think you could change the trajectory of African American contemporary literature. You've got the makings of what Brandon calls 'a real Black writer.' I'm so excited about the new projects you're working on. If you sign with Chatham Ward, we'll have our lawyers get you out of the deal with Nathalie in the next week or so, and Brandon says he can get us half the advance in three weeks. I'll be in touch."

You never contacted Nathalie, but a few days later, Bobbie, the perfect agent/fine sister did. "Nathalie is so fucking pissed," she said a few days later, "but all's fair in love, war, and business." As you wondered whether this was love, war, or business, you and your perfect agent/fine sister waited and waited and waited for Brandon to deliver.

Six months later, three months after your initial publication date of June 2009, Brandon offered you substantially less money than he promised and a publication date two years later than the one he had verbally agreed to.

"Pardon me for saying this," your perfect agent said over the phone from a different 212 number, "but Brandon Farley is a bona fide bitch-ass nigga for fucking us out of thousands of dollars and pushing the pub date back to June 2011. He's just not professional.

I'm wondering if this was just some ploy to get you away from KenteKloth. He's been trying to take all his authors away from there as a way of fucking the company."

"I don't get it," you said, shamefully excited that your agent used *fucking, bitch-ass,* and *nigga* in one conversation.

"So Brandon acquired this wonderful list of new literary Black authors at KenteKloth, and they were all going to work with Nathalie after he was basically fired from the company. Nathalie and the house were going to get credit for a lot of his work. Do you get it now? We got caught up in something really nasty."

You got your first edit letter from Brandon Farley in July 2011. In addition to telling you that the tone of the piece was far too dark and that you needed an obvious redemptive ending, Brandon wrote, "There's way too much racial politics in this piece, bro. You're writing to a multicultural society, but you're not writing multiculturally."

You wondered out loud what writing "multiculturally" actually meant and what kind of Black man would write the word *bro* in an e-mail.

"Bro, we need this book to come down from 284 pages to 150," he said. "We're going to have to push the pub date back again, too. I'm thinking June 2012. Remember," he wrote, "it's business. I think you should start from scratch but keep the spirit. Does the narrator really need to be a Black boy? Does the story really need to take place in Mississippi? The Percy Jackson demographic," he wrote. "That's a big part of the audience for your novel. Read it over the weekend. Real Black writers adjust to the market, bro, at least for their first novels."

By the time you found out Percy Jackson wasn't the name of a

conflicted Black boy from Birmingham but a fake-ass Harry Potter
who saved the gods of Mount Olympus, you were already broken.
Someone you claimed to love told you that you were letting your
publishing failure turn you into a monster. She said you were becoming the kind of human being you always despised. You defended yourself against the truth and really against responsibility,
as American monsters and American murderers tend to do, and
you tried to make this person feel as absolutely worthless, confused, and malignant as you were. Later that night, you couldn't
sleep, and instead of diving back into the fiction, for the first time in
your life, you wrote the sentence, "I've been slowly killing myself
and others close to me just like my uncle."

Something else was wrong, too. Your body no longer felt like
your body, and you doubted whether your grandma would ever see
your work before one of you died.

Two years after the first pub date for your first book, there was
no book. Questions fell like dominoes.

*Why would Brandon buy the book?* you kept asking yourself. "Why
would that bitch-ass nigga get you out of a contract for a book
he didn't want?" your perfect agent kept asking you. "Why'd you
promise stuff you couldn't deliver?" you asked Brandon on the
phone.

"The book doesn't just have Duck Duck Goose's name on it,"
you told him, slightly aware of what happens when keeping it real
goes wrong. "My name is on that shit, too. That means, on some
level, it ain't business. I feel like you want me to lie. I read and write
for a living, Brandon. I see the shit that's out there. I've read your
other books. I see your goofy book covers looking like greasy children's menus at Applebee's. I ain't putting my name on a fucking

greasy Applebee's menu. I'm not. Don't front like it's about quality. You and maybe your editorial board don't think you can sell this book because you don't believe Black southern audiences read literary shit. And that's fine. Maybe you're right. If you didn't believe in it, why buy it in the first place? Look, I can create an audience for this novel with these essays I've been writing," you tell him. "It sounds stupid, but I can. I just need to know that you're committed to really publishing this book. Do you believe in the vision or not?"

After a long pause where you could hear Brandon telling his assistant, Jacques, to leave the room and get him a warm bear claw with extra glaze, he said, "Bro, you're the second person to complain to me this morning about how I do my job. The first person had a bit more tact. Honestly," he said, "reading your work has been painful. It's business. Take that folksy shit back to Mississippi. I did you a favor. Don't forget that. You're just not a good writer, bro. Good-bye."

The next morning you got an e-mail from Brandon with the following message:

Hey Wanda,

I finished the revision this afternoon. It totally kicks ass. Congrats. I've sent back a few line edits, but it's brilliant. Move over Teju and Chimamanda. There's a new African writer on the scene showing these Black American writers how it's done. I'm so proud of you. Always darkest before the dawn, Wanda. It feels so empowering to work with the future of contemporary diasporic literature.

                                    Tell David hi for me. Best,
                                    Brandon

Your name was not, and never will be, "Wanda."

You logged into your Facebook feed and found that Brandon, your Facebook friend, had posted the covers of recently published and forthcoming books he'd edited. Wanda's book and all the other covers really looked like greasy children's menus at Applebee's. Your eyes watered as you Googled the published authors Brandon had signed two years after you. You wanted your name on an Applebee's menu, too.

Even though you were fatter than you'd ever been and the joints in your hip got rustier and more decayed every day, parts of you were a rider. Yeah, Brandon bombed first, you thought, but right there, you felt determined to get your novel out by any means necessary so you could thank him in the acknowledgments:

... And a special thanks to that shape-shifting cowardly ol' lying ass, Brandon Farley, the untrustworthy editing-cause-he-can't-write-a-lick ass Tom who'd sell out his mama for a gotdamn glazed bear claw as long as the bear claw had been half eaten by a white librarian named Jacques or Percy Jackson. I know where you live. And I got goons. Can you see me now? Goooood. Congrats, BRO.

Instead you wrote:

Not sure why you sent that e-mail intended for Wanda Onga-Nana, Brandon. I hope we both appreciate the distinction between what's marketable and what's possible. Glad you're having success with some of your authors. I

think you should give my books a chance to breathe, too.
Thanks for the inspiration. Tell Wanda congratulations.


Brandon never responded to your e-mail.

You stayed in your bedroom for weeks writing essays to your
dead uncle, your grandma, the son and daughter you didn't have.
Outside that bedroom, and outside of your writing life, you'd fully
become a liar, unafraid to say I love you, too willing to say I'm sorry,
unwilling to change the ingredients of your life, which meant you'd
gobbled up your heart and you were halfway done gobbling up the
heart of a woman who loved you.

You'd become typical.

One Tuesday near the end of spring, you couldn't move your left
leg or feel your toes and you'd been sweating through your mattress
for a month. You knew there was something terribly wrong years
before your furry-fingered doctor, with tiny hands and eyebrows to
die for, used the words "malignant growth."

"It won't be easy," the doctor told you the Friday before spring
break. "You're the second person I've diagnosed with this today, but
there's still a chance we can get it without surgery. You said you've
been living with the pain for three years? Frankly, I'm worried about
you," the doctor said. "You seem like you're holding something in.
Fear is okay, you know? Do you have any questions?"

You watched the doctor's eyebrows sway like black wheat. They
looked like a hyper four-year-old had gone buck wild with a fistful
of black crayons. "I like your eyebrows," you told the doctor. "I don't
know what's wrong with me. I just want my grandma to think I'm a
real writer."

"I'd actually like to recommend therapy in addition to the treatment," the doctor told you before he walked you out the door.

For the next few months you took the treatment he gave you and prided yourself on skipping the therapy. You told no one about the malignant growth in your hip, not even the person whose heart you were eating. Though you could no longer run or trust, you could eat and you could hate. So you ate, and you ate, and you hated, until sixty-eight pounds and five months later, you were finally unrecognizable to yourself.

You accepted, on a ride through Georgia that ended with you falling asleep and crashing your car, that you had sprinted away from the hard work of being the human being and writer you wanted to be. Like every hater you've ever known, you shielded yourself from critique and obsessed with wading in the funk of how people had done you wrong.

One Sunday near the end of spring, after talking to your two family members who were both killing themselves slowly, too, you made the decision to finally show the world the blues you'd been creating. You also decided to finish revising the novel without Brandon.

"The whole time I'd been in those woods," you wrote in one of the last scenes in the book, "I'd never stopped and looked up."

You spent the next four months of your life skipping treatments for your hip and getting a new draft of the novel done. You didn't dumb down the story for Brandon, for multiculturalism, or for school boards you'd never see. You wrote an honest book to Paul Beatty, Margaret Walker Alexander, Cassandra Wilson, Big K.R.I.T., Octavia Butler, Gangsta Boo, your little cousins, and all your teachers.

You prayed on it and sent the book to Brandon. You told him that you had created a post-Katrina, Afrofuturist, time-travel-ish, Black southern love story filled with adventure, metafiction, and mystery. You wanted to call the book *Long Division*, after two of the characters' insistence on showing their work in the past, present, and future.

"It's a book I'm proud of," you wrote in the letter attached to the manuscript. "It's something I needed to read when I was a teenager in Mississippi. Shit, it's something I need to read now. I'm willing to work on it. Just let me know if you get the vision."

Brandon responded the same day that he would check it out over the weekend and get back to you with his thoughts.

Four months later, he finally sent an e-mail: "Ultimately, the same problems exist in this draft that were in the other drafts." Brandon ended the e-mail:

> We need more traditional adventure. We need to know less about the relationships between the characters, less racial politics, and more about the adventure. You need to explain how the science fiction works, bro. No one is going to believe Black kids from Mississippi traveling through time talking about institutional racism. It's way too meandering. Kill the metafictive angle. You haven't earned the right to pull that off. This is still painful. I'm convinced you really do not want to be a real Black writer, bro. The success of your book will be partially dependent on readers who have a different sensibility than your intended audience . . .

Still too ashamed to really reckon with your disease or your failures and too cowardly to own your decisions, you stretched your legs out on the floor of your living room and cried your eyes out. After crying, laughing, and wondering if love really could save all the people public policy forgot, you grabbed a pad and scribbled, "Alone, you sit on the floor. . . ."

After writing for about two hours, you wonder why you start the piece with "Alone, you . . ." You are the "I" to no one in the world, not even yourself.

You've eviscerated people who loved you when they made you the second person in their lives, when they put the relationship's needs ahead of your wants. And you've been eviscerated for the same thing.

You're not a monster. You're not innocent.

You look down at the browning S key on your keyboard. You don't know how long you'll live. No one does. You don't know how long you'll have two legs. You know that it's time to stop letting your anger and hate toward Brandon Farley and your publishing failure be more important than the art of being human and healthy. You know it's time to admit to yourself, your writing, and folks who love you that you're at least the second person to feel like you're really good at slowly killing yourself and others in America.

"Sorry your reads have been so painful, Brandon," you start typing.

I want to get healthy. That means not only that I need to be honest; it also means I've got to take my life back and move to a place where I no longer blame you for failure. I've thought and said some terrible things about you. I've blamed you for the breaking of my body and the breaking of my heart. I hate the word *bitch* but I've used it so many times in my head when I'm thinking about you. Women deserve better. You deserve better. I really believed that you and your approval would determine whether or not I was a real Black writer, worthy of real self-respect and real dignity.

There was something in my work, something in me that resonated with your work and something in you. We are connected. I'm not sure what happens next. No young writer, real or not, leaves an iconic press before their first book comes, right? Whatever. I can't put my name on the book that you want written and it's apparent that you won't put your company's name on the book I want read. We tried, Brandon, but life is long and short. I've written my way out of death and destruction before. I'm trying to do it again. I think I'm done with the New York publishing thing for a while. I'm through with the editors, the agents, and all that stress. No hate at all. It's just not for me. I can't be healthy dealing with all that stuff. I'll get my work out to my folks and if they want more, I'll show them. If not, that's fine. I'm a writer. I write.

I'm sorry and sorrier that sorry is rarely enough. God gave me senses and a little bit of health. It's time for me to use them the best that I can. Thanks for the shot. Good luck. I hope you like the work I'm doing.

Not sure if it's good, but I know it's Black, blue, Mississippi, and honest. I'm not a bro, Brandon. You ain't either. Thanks again for everything.

You look up.

You close your eyes.

You breathe.

You look down and you keep on writing, revising, reading, reckoning, working . . . because that's what real Black writers do.

## Reading Suggestions

Robert Jones Jr., *The Prophets*

Deeshaw Philyaw, *The Secret Lives of Church Ladies*

Derrick Harriell, *Come Kingdom*

Imani Perry, *South to America: A Journey Below the Mason-Dixon Line to Understand the Soul of a Nation*

David J. Dennis Jr. in collaboration with David J. Dennis Sr., *The Movement Made Us: A Father, a Son, and the Legacy of a Freedom Ride*

# On Political Fiction and Fictional Politics

*Mohammed Hanif*

**My older brother, who passed away in 2021, used to** joke that there was no point to writing a book if your own family couldn't read it. Although notionally college-educated, he couldn't read my first novel because it was in English. I considered that to be an advantage. The novel had too many cusswords, extended political jokes about soldiers and religious scholars, and a tastefully done boy-on-boy sex scene. I thought it a blessing that my family couldn't read my novel and judge me for the filth in my mind.

My brother wasn't the only one curious about *A Case of Exploding Mangoes*. A childhood friend and connoisseur of world literature in Urdu also kept haranguing me about my novel. Was it more like García Márquez or Kafka? Had I gone the Chekhov way or was I still trying to mimic Dostoevsky? Not getting any clear answers from me, he insisted I should immediately get it translated into Urdu, and why hadn't I written it in Urdu anyway?

Although I write in Urdu and in my mother tongue Punjabi as well, it was quite obvious to me that I would write a novel in English for the simple reason that most of the novels that had captured my imagination happened to be in English. Originally written in Spanish or Persian or Russian or even Hindi, they were available to me only in English. Also, my novel was mostly set in military cantonments and air force bases where the language of war and love is English and everyone can express a range of emotions in about fifty words mostly revolving around genitalia, not the kind of language I wanted my own family to read. We spoke Punjabi at home and Urdu at school. It was obvious to me that you could say things in Urdu that you couldn't in English. Similarly, you could write stuff in English that would get you in trouble if stated in Urdu. I learned my English in the Pakistan Air Force, where "motherfucker" was a term of endearment, while its Urdu equivalent was a serious insult.

A *Case of Exploding Mangoes* features a dead military dictator, some living generals, and a horny Saudi prince. I kept their real names but made them live and die as I, the writer, pleased. I was orchestrating the mechanics of the assassination of a brutal military dictator. In our culture we are often told that we shouldn't speak ill of the dead, but what do you do if the dead is pure evil? Before publishing I showed the manuscript to a couple of journalist friends in Pakistan, and their first reaction was horror: *What the hell are you thinking?* Then came the sane advice that I should change the names of my characters. But I had spent too much time with these names, and it seemed like an act of betrayal to give them up. I had been a journalist long enough to know that we hacks are alarmists by profession. I reminded my journalist friends, and myself, that the cover clearly identified it as a novel, and on the third page was the disclaimer, drafted by English lawyers, that it's a work of fiction and any resemblance to people alive or dead is just a beautiful coincidence.

When the novel came out, the world didn't stop revolving on its axis. I was nervous about the reaction in Pakistan, especially after my Pakistani publisher backed out. They had booked a banquet hall in a posh hotel, drawn up a guest list, and decided on a high tea menu for the launch, but at the last moment, their printer told them that he couldn't possibly publish my book on the same presses he used to print holy texts. I had never realized that the printers actually read what they print. The Indian edition of the book had to be imported to Pakistan—it didn't cause any harm to our national security vis-à-vis India.

The novel was a seasonal hit, and I became a minor celebrity at literary festivals and reading circles. I was pleasantly surprised when young people turned up to the readings, eleven-year-olds accompanied by their parents who boasted that their child had finished the book in one sitting. Soon I realized that many of the readers were not reading my novel as fiction but as an episode from our history. The most common questions were how much of my book was fact and how much fiction and how I knew all these top-secret events from our past. I would always say that on a certain day, a plane took off from an airbase and exploded a few minutes later. That was the only historical fact. The rest I made up. *A Case of Exploding Mangoes* features, among other weird things, a poison-tipped sword, a crow carrying a blind woman's curse, and the life cycle of tapeworms. I was amused that people could take my flights of fancy as historical events, but maybe that says more about our idea of history than my craft.

I had a scary moment at a reading when a former chief of Pakistan's Inter-Services Intelligence—which features in the novel in all its glory—put his arm around my shoulder, took me to a corner, and said, "Son, you have written a fine book, now tell me, who are your sources?" While researching this novel I had read a few hagiographies about my central character, which portrayed him as a dull, god-fearing, humble man. This was not only a lie but of no use to a fiction writer. I had consulted astrological charts that claimed to have predicted his demise. Having spent some time learning to fly, I already knew what it felt like when a plane went out of control. I also knew how to put on a military uniform and what to do with a ceremonial sword. I tried to convince the intelligence chief that although I knew the texture of military life, I had made up the story, but he gave me a knowing smile as if we were now both in on a national conspiracy.

Many western reviewers and interviewers obsessed about a brief love scene between two trainee officers. "Are you saying there is homosexuality in the Pakistani army?" one interviewer pointedly asked me. "Is there homosexuality in the British army?" I asked instead. I felt a bit queasy and then a bit smug for having averted a direct answer to the question. If I claimed that there was homosexuality in my country's military, I would be lynched, but if I fictionalized a tender moment between two boys, I might get away with it. In Pakistan, nobody bothered about that passage, two young boys swimming in their own testosterone, trouble in the barracks, what were the boys going to do?

A pair of young men cornered me after a reading and thanked me for writing that paragraph. I said it was a plot device. One of them shyly volunteered that sometimes they read that passage together and then reenacted it in bed. I almost choked on my coffee and said that they should be careful, it was a novel and not a sex manual.

\* \* \*

At the time of the novel's English publication, I believed I had more than enough political reasons for not having the book translated into Urdu. And what would my brother think if he read that scene? At the same time, it began to feel like an act of cowardice when others pointed out that it was all very well to write a novel like this for an English-speaking elite, but why couldn't people read their own story in their own language? My friend suggested that since my Urdu wasn't bad, I should translate it myself. I reasoned that if I tried to do so, I might end up writing an entirely different, probably more family-friendly, book. Then another friend started to translate it but, after working on a couple of chapters, died in a road accident. I convinced myself that the whole business of Urdu translation was cursed.

A young poet and brilliant translator, Kashif Raza, approached me with a translation proposal. I didn't quite know how to say no, so I said yes, hoping that he would become busy with a more important project. Within three months I had an Urdu manuscript one hundred pages longer than the English text sitting at my table, daring me to see the work of my mind in the language that is spoken around me. For weeks, I couldn't bring myself to read it.

Finally, when I read it, it sounded like the book I had written, faithful to the original but also full of Urdu and Punjabi flourishes. It was also slightly smuttier than it had seemed in English. I realized for the first time that although I had written my story in English, a lot of it had been conceived in Urdu and Punjabi. Many of the descriptions and dialogue came into sharper focus in the translation. Raza had pulled down the veil of English language, and suddenly, it was all there, in bright sunlight; the smells were stronger, the insults more insulting, the intimate moments a bit more poetic.

I gave it to my world literature enthusiast friend and, for the first and last time, he said something nice to me: "It reads like a proper novel. You should write another one. And better write in Urdu."

Now that I had that stamp of approval, I thought I couldn't possibly censor myself by not publishing it.

I approached Pakistan's largest Urdu publisher with the manuscript. I had recommendations from two famous Urdu writers. "He can't say no to an author recommended by me," the grand old man of Urdu fiction, Abdulla Hussain, told me. "Half his sales are from my books." My novel was accepted for publication with some enthusiasm and referred to an editorial board, a group of unnamed scholars apparently asked to vet the manuscript for any possible offensive material. I didn't hear from the publishers for a couple of years, but I was in that happy position where I could tell my family and friends that the Urdu translation was with the publishers. Any day now, I kept saying. After two years I made a polite inquiry, and the publisher told me that it was almost ready for publication and did I have any ideas for the book cover because they didn't want to use the original cover. I approached an artist friend who overnight came up with a stunning idea, which my publisher approved. For another year and a half I didn't hear anything.

I decided to visit my publisher's headquarters, based in one of the largest bookshops in Lahore, sometimes called the cultural capital of Pakistan. It was thrilling to walk into that shop and see all the Urdu books I had loved growing up lining its shelves. I was excited to be joining this great company. But the publisher himself seemed reluctant to let my novel sit with these luminaries. The editorial board, he told me, had some reservations. I was open to editorial suggestions and ready to submit to national sensitivities. "Please share their editorial notes and I'll consider them. It's a work of fiction, not a sacred text. I don't want to get anybody into trouble," I said. He refused to share their objections and said, "Look, you live here, you're a journalist, you know what they can object to." I was not only being asked to censor my own work but also to figure out what to censor. Here, I gave him my best and, in retrospect, a desperate sales pitch. "The book has been out for ten years and nobody has objected to it. It's part of the school curriculum, it's being taught in universities," I boasted. "And if you are worried about the military types, many of them have read the book and they all love it." That was an exaggeration. Only two of my former colleagues in the air force had acknowledged the existence of this book. One of them said he loved my "naughty" book, but added, "I wondered if it should be in my squadron's library but decided against it because I don't want to corrupt young officers' minds."

My publisher was a major supplier to military libraries. "I do a lot of business with these people," he said. "Sometimes it takes them a decade to get the joke." We parted on a let's-wait-and-see note. Somebody who knew the publisher told me he had been as clear as he was going to be about rejecting the translation of my novel. "This is a big, fat Lahori No," I was told.

It would turn out that the publisher who didn't quite say no to my book despite sitting on the translation for four and a half years wasn't joking when he said that sometimes it takes the military ten years to get a joke.

A small, legendary publisher in Karachi said yes to the translation. My publisher and editor Hoori Noorani published it with a lot of professionalism, love, and fearless passion. She worked hard on polishing the manuscript but didn't cut a single line from the original. After the Urdu edition was published, we went back to literary festivals and reading circles. Some people passionately objected to the Urdu title. Too literal, they said; too clunky. The double entendre in "Case" in *A Case of Exploding Mangoes* was lost in the Urdu translation. Readers kept suggesting catchier, more poetic titles. It was a bit irritating, but we took comfort in the fact that readers were so invested in the book that they took the translated title personally. We told them the joke about the military's delayed reactions to a joke, and we sold many books.

The audience that my translator and I met in our Urdu readings had a slightly different take. They enjoyed the jokes, they asked about fact and fiction, but some of them also raised doubts about whether one was allowed to present real people in such a macabre way. Was a writer allowed to rewrite our history? Was it against our cultural norms to make fun of the dead? It was quite clear that some things that were acceptable, even admirable, in the English text had become points of debate in Urdu. Outside Pakistan the novel was read as a political thriller about a "third-world" country, but in Pakistan, it was interpreted as an attempt to take on the legacy of a brutal dictator. I was asked if the late general was all that bad, or whether I had written a revenge novel.

These exchanges with the audience were polite. We kept pointing out the cover with the word *novel* on it. My translator, who had almost given up on me and my book, was happy to see his labor of love being acknowledged. He is a poet and a broadcaster, and he read his favorite passages with dramatic flourish and had the audience in stitches. We also said wise things about the importance of translation.

At last, my brother asked me for a copy, and I told him that if my family wouldn't buy my book, who would? For the first time in his life, he bought a novel. On a visit home, I saw it on his side table. I didn't have the heart to ask him what he made of it. Then he said, "I gave up after a few pages. It's all lies, isn't it?" I was disappointed but consoled myself by saying that if he hadn't read a novel in his entire life, he couldn't very well start in his seventies. And while Pakistan has a strong culture of oral storytelling, the idea of a grown-up man sitting down to make up a story is still considered a bit frivolous. I was relieved that my brother had given up before he got to the dirty bits. A friend of his borrowed it from him and, last I heard, was still liking it despite "all the lies in it."

Eight months after the publication of the Urdu translation, someone finally got the joke. In real life General Muhammad Zia-ul-Haq died in a plane crash, but the nation never found out if it was an accident or assassination. There were dozens of theories about who might have killed him and how. In my novel I borrowed from these conspiracy theories, invented some of my own, and retold the jokes people made up during the dictator's regime to ridicule him. Ijaz-ul-Haq, the son of the late dictator General Zia-ul-Haq, served us with a one-billion-rupee defamation notice. His contention was that by writing and circulating this book we had defamed his father. The notice came with seventeen-page-long excerpts culled from the Urdu translation. It seemed as if someone with an obscene mind had gone through the book and, with alarming accuracy, pulled out all the dirty bits from my novel. A friendly lawyer offered to fight the case pro bono and promised a lot of excitement. "Can a notorious dead military dictator be defamed? We'll ask the political prisoners who were tortured on his orders to come and testify," he said. I requested our reply point out that the English version of the book had been in circulation for a decade without offending the son. Could the late father be defamed only in Urdu? My lawyer rejected my suggestion and said we would stick to the this-is-a-work-of-fiction defense. I had spent enough time in journalism to know that when in trouble with courts, it was best to forget your literary pretentions and listen to your lawyer, but in this case literary pretension was in itself going to be our defense.

While we were drafting the reply to the defamation letter, men who said they were from the ISI descended on my publisher's office and confiscated all the books without showing any official order to do so. They also secured the lists of booksellers who had bought the book. There were midnight knocks on the door of my publisher's house. They went to her manager's house and harassed him. In what seemed like coordinated raids, they came to two major bookshops and confiscated all the copies and bizarrely asked for the names and contacts of the people who had bought the book. Suddenly nobody was laughing at the joke.

We made some noise on social media, the international wires picked up the story, writers' and journalists' organizations condemned it. The ISI denied in public that it had conducted the raids, but a mediator purportedly from the agency asked us to meet up to clear the air. I met a one-star general who said he had ordered the raids. He was almost apologetic and said that he was only carrying out his orders. "We didn't touch the English book, right?" he tried to reassure me. Then he told me his theory about why he was asked to confiscate the Urdu edition. "When your book came out ten years ago, it was quite fashionable," he said. "Even I used to carry a copy to show off." He didn't say that he had read the book, but the idea of my novel as a fashion accessory was pleasing to me. "But when you read the same things in Urdu, it can be a bit disturbing for people," he said. I became certain that he hadn't read either the Urdu or English version of my novel. "You know there is that scene where the Saudi crown prince is buggering our late president. In English, it was amusing. In Urdu it's a bit disturbing," he said. I was scared. I didn't have the heart to tell him that no Saudi buggers our president in my book. Later, I thought, maybe the young general has more creative filth in his mind than I ever did.

## Reading Suggestions

Hanif Kureishi, *Dreaming and Scheming*

Saadat Hasan Manto, *Ganjay Farishtay* (essays in Urdu)

Mario Vargas Llosa, *Aunt Julia and the Scriptwriter*

Abdullah Hussein, *Udaas Naslain* (The Weary Generations)

Ismat Chughtai, *The Quilt*

# On Reception and Resilience

*Sharlene Teo*

**My first novel came out four years ago riding a wave** of buzz generated by kind words from fellow writers, good timing, and a striking cover. That year I felt like a bridal birthday debutante, fizzing with hopeful excitement that always hovered on the knife-edge of catastrophic failure. Yet to be more vocal about those anxieties at the time seemed glib or entitled because I recognized that it was a privilege and a miracle even to get to that juncture. 2018, pre-pandemic, feels like such a long time ago, and now, with the distance of hindsight, I am more able to reflect upon my experiences.

That year I learned firsthand that in the circuitous, complex life and afterlife of a manuscript—from the moment editors acquired my book to prepublication publicity—the most control I had was during the drafting and editing stage. Everything else was governed by luck and chance and mysterious discussions between industry people. I did not realize that any form of publicity was a blessing, not a given, for a debut novelist. Back then I didn't know—and I still don't—much about the logistics of window displays or shelf space. I was just grateful for my book to have a place at the table in stores.

Often it was alongside other debuts. Sometimes it was laid out on a table of books that seemed to have no thematic similarities except that they were by nonwhite people. To be grouped under a homogenizing otherness seemed better than not being counted at all.

It's tempting to be hawkishly online during the publication of your debut in order to gain some semblance of insight into the opaque, rarefied process that is mainstream publishing. I didn't have the willpower to avoid my own reviews; hunting for an ego stroke, instead stumbling across some thorny critique or snarky comment that lingered in my consciousness for days afterward because it confirmed some insecurity I harbored about my own writing. Such self-sleuthing is narcissistic and rarely ends well; the internet becomes a toxic Pandora's Box varnished in shame and self-indulgence. I was a heavy Twitter user and checked Goodreads compulsively, watching the good—and bad—reviews accumulate. Surprisingly, it was not the one-star zingers that stung the most but the three-star ones, the readers who spent time with the book and at the end of it thought, "meh." I couldn't separate readerly experience from the maelstrom of feelings and effort that went into writing that novel. When someone really enjoyed it, I felt thrilled and warmed and moved. Dismissals felt like not being seen, a repudiation of what I had intensely tried to communicate through the story. Of course, it sounds irrational to take negative or indifferent receptions of a book personally. Naively, I wanted everyone to love it, even though it was flawed.

After a while my monitoring grew wearying and unsustainable. It did not do my mental health any good. Sapped of creative energy and too self-consciously online, I lacked the stamina to write fiction while publicizing my book at the same time. Discussing my debut while trying to write felt like trying to date someone new while constantly rehashing the convolutions of a former relationship onstage and online. In 2019 I left Twitter, wincing at the small blue bird. I stopped checking Goodreads. I kept Instagram, though. I liked how I could streamline my puppy-and-meme-filled feed and dip a toe into the book world on my own terms. I've heard from friends with recent book deals that maintaining a social media presence is baked into their contracts. That it becomes almost a second job to repost and retweet and thank everyone for mentions. I sound cynical about social media but must add that hypocritically, I'm on Instagram daily: it does have the potential for delight and positive connections, professionally and personally. To have no social media at all seems to be the province of the invincibly established, famous, or very confident: it's a baller move, a rejection of self-publicity and the need to update strangers with a constant stream of hot takes or cultural recommendations. It connotes innate confidence in the analogue force of your own interests, an admirable disengagement from the churning attention deficit nonlogic of the internet in which image postures as intimacy and novelty postures as connectedness.

Sometimes I get a nice email or message from a reader; I receive this with gratitude and a growing detachment. It's out of my hands, that first one. Now that enough time has passed, I don't feel any immediate pressure to complete my second novel quickly. As a result, I worry and wonder if I ever will. Difficult Second Novel Syndrome, Difficult Second Album Syndrome . . . all names for the sophomore slump that makes a creative person suspect the first one was a fluke. A terrifying amnesia occurs; I don't know how I did it, finished something that satisfied enough to be sold. Yet now I'm unsure where to go, what to do. The terrain of the land of books is constantly shifting. Fads come and go. I hate how the intuitive and messy creative process of drafting a manuscript is now inflected, to me, with the cold, calculated language of commerce and salability. For as long as I can remember, I've wanted to write books for the rest of my life: why, then, do I find writing so hard and complain about it all the time?

That debut was my baby; my relationship to it was so personal and emotional—I wanted everyone to coo over my paper flesh and blood, this bound culmination of my lifelong efforts and fascinations. It was the first wild pancake from my imagination: messy and imperfect. I flung everything close to hand in it, all those feelings and impressions from the tunneling trenches of childhood through to adolescence. Singapore, my home country, was a huge part of the book, and I felt most apprehensive about how it would be received at home, if fellow Singaporeans would find its representation worthy and true. Such a loaded cluster of words—"representation," "worthy," "true."

In *Writing the Other: A Practical Approach,* Nisi Shawl and Cynthia Ward describe "the unmarked state" as "the default state for any character otherwise not described . . . white, male, heterosexual, single, young, and physically able. Other characteristics people have noted include possessing a mid-level income, childless, and human."

The burden of representation increases the more you deviate from that state. In 2020 I wrote a draft of a novel that swerved away from the politics of any representation, which centered Singaporeans without naming their nationality and contained no indicators of place; it was a technical and narrative failure. I rewrote a hundred pages of it with more conventional settings established and found myself bored by my own story. Stripped of its gimmicks, it was barely bones. I'm often struck by what Beth Loffreda and Claudia Rankine have to say in *The Racial Imaginary: Writers on Race in the Life of the Mind* about the expectation placed on writers of color to write a story with "universal" resonance:

> If we continue to think the "universal" as better than, as the pinnacle, we will always discount writing that doesn't look universal because it accounts for race or some other de- meaned category. . . . We are captive, still, to the style of championing literature that says works by writers of color succeed when a white person can nevertheless relate to it— that it "transcends" its category. To say that a book by a writer of color is great because it transcends its particularity to say something "human" (and we've all read that review, maybe written it ourselves) is to reveal the racist underpin- ning quite clearly: such a claim begins from the stance that people of color are not human, only achieve the human in certain circumstances.

Yet despite the conditional acclaim accorded to stories of "uni- versal" resonance, writers of color are also expected to deliver illu- minating ethnographic data about where they *really* come from. As Elaine Castillo puts it, readers "end up going to writers of color to learn the specific—and go to white writers to feel the universal." This distinction between learning and feeling is a crucial one; it connotes that novels by writers of color have an instructive, educa- tional, or touristic quality.

* * *

At nineteen I moved from Singapore to England for university. Academic immigration is a privilege—I keep falling back to and referring to this word *privilege*, an anticipatory term that indicates at the very least some form of self-awareness. I've lived in London now for close to thirteen years, and I feel comfortable in this smog-choked, messy city, but I rarely write fiction set in it. I always give the excuse that there are more than enough books about London. But perhaps it's a failure of my imagination, an inability to enliven the details that are alarmingly close to me. My fiction almost always takes place in Singapore, the place of my birth that each year grows ever more sublime and remote. My characters are almost always Chinese Singaporeans. Singapore is an intrinsic part of me, but the Singapore in my imagination becomes, over time, increasingly that— a vector of imagination, like the life-size replica of New York in the 2008 Charlie Kaufman film *Synecdoche, New York*. The soundstage city shifts and warps, grows gargantuan, harshly lit.

When I visit home, I'm confronted by the growing gulf between what I remember and what I no longer know. Shame-struck by my own touristic tendencies, I take pictures, I make notes. But I rarely use them when I'm writing. The Singapore in my imagination melts into an emotional, subconscious landscape, dream architecture hewing to the mumbled, sentimental half-logic of the stories we tell ourselves about how we came to be. Memory is an eerie, vital realm scripted in the faint but indelible font of our earliest daydreams and disappointments.

I have spent the last two years trying to finish my second novel; at the time of writing this essay I have put it aside, perhaps for good. It wasn't working. I'm starting from scratch. If I see someone who published their debut at the same time or even after me launch their second or possibly third book, something inside me shrieks like one of the doomed teenagers in *Final Destination,* and then I chuck that fear aside because if I'm not careful it could grow into bitterness. It's both creatively pointless and psychologically harmful to measure your progress against anyone else's. This isn't to discount how naturally that comparative reflex comes to us—it's drummed into our brains via the ambient derogatory hum of late capitalism and a scarcity mindset. Commercial comparison is, after all, part of the blurb-and-buzz-making business. As a writer of color, you will invariably get compared to another writer from the same broad region, or a far more accomplished and famous writer to try and excite their fans, or another person writing a threateningly similar-sounding book. Perhaps one day this could be different, and each book will be received simply as itself and on its own terms, but I don't think we're there yet.

As a female writer of color, I have been mistaken countless times for other Asian female writers. At a book launch once, no fewer than eight people came up to me assuming I was the Japanese illustrator of a book cover. They didn't even ask; they just assumed. My last name has been misspelled and mispronounced very often too, but I minimize these experiences; I don't want to be seen as a complainer, I want to give people the benefit of the doubt because it takes up less energy than being angry and exasperated. And I grapple with postcolonial double consciousness: both minority (in the U.K.) and majority (in Singapore), trying, in my fiction, not to pander to a white gaze nor compromise an identity position that has never felt all that stable nor simple to me in the first place.

I think a novel is a book-length exploration of what a writer is curious or obsessed about in the world. I think a novel is a book-length question that doesn't always have a clear or easy answer. The most helpful things I've learned over the past few years are to protect my inner life, avoid chasing likes and tractions, and to forget about obsessively monitoring the reception of my own work. Once it's out there, it's no longer my business. I have learned when to follow an idea and when to let it go. When I'm struck by too much self-doubt, I read some beautiful fiction. It reminds me of why I started writing in the first place—because of my mad love of fiction and its empathetic possibilities, the way it makes us think and feel. It's the opposite of isolating, this communion between reader and writer that spans continents, decades, time zones.

The main responsibility I feel in writing is to be attentive to how the contours of my own identity and experience map into my imagination, bearing in mind there are so many different ways of seeing and being in the world. Each in their own specific manners wonderful and valid and difficult. I can't speak for everyone else. I can only be as frank and honest in where the fiction is coming from as possible and hope that the reader recognizes something true in my story. That in the small world of a sentence, they feel something real.

I used to think it was better for a book to be hated than unmemorable, but now I'm not so sure. I don't think I will ever write a book that everyone loves. And I've made peace with the fact that I can't please everyone and that the story-shaped impulses and ideas I harbor will never live up to their reality. Some days I tire myself out just feeling bad about not writing and feeling shabby and inadequate. But I remind myself right now: it's okay to worry that I'm not writing enough nor capable of finishing anything, to worry that I'm getting worse at articulating myself and creating complex characters. Worry is part of my process, perhaps. Failure too—language often fails me. But that's the joy of it, paraphrasing what Joan Didion observed somewhere about writing being a not-knowing, a thinking-through. I love this form of thinking through. What matters most is trying. And I'll keep trying.

*Reading Suggestions*

Matthew Salesses, *Craft in the Real World: Rethinking
    Fiction Writing and Workshopping*
Elaine Castillo, *How to Read Now*
Alexander Chee, *How to Write an Autobiographical Novel*
Cathy Park Hong, *Minor Feelings: An Asian American
    Reckoning*

# On the Ideal Conditions for Writing

*Deepa Anappara*

"Language is a peculiar destiny."
—Tishani Doshi, "A Fable for the 21st Century,"
*Girls Are Coming Out of the Woods*

1.

**My sister is dying of cancer, and I am writing a novel.**
I can rearrange these words, alter the tense or syntax, but it won't
make the sentence any less disagreeable or coarse. I can't accept,
much less articulate, this reality. Outside the hospital where my
sister is receiving treatment I walk on roads that lack pavements,
the wheels of bikes and cars rasping at my heels. Grief is the un-
sightly red patch thickening my right eyelid, the persistent nausea
that exaggerates the feeling that beneath my skin I'm entirely hol-
low. On my shoulders are the red rut marks imprinted by the straps
of a backpack that holds chargers, adapters, a laptop, batteries,
medicines, books, an e-reader, and a journal divided into two un-
equal halves. Scribbled on the journal's first few pages are notes
about my novel written before my sister's diagnosis. Whatever the
condition of writing I imagined when I underlined Scenes and
Myth, it was not this. Now, time ripples, buckles, dissolves, surges
past the margins as I attempt to pin it down with to-do lists. *Talk to
doctor about PET-CT results. Scan documents. Send biopsy report to M.
Speak to V about insurance. Call wig guy. Ask S to transfer money.* After I

have put a tick mark against some of these tasks, I sit on a flimsy plastic chair in the hospital room, several browser tabs and a Word document that I call my novel open on my laptop. Voices and feet shuffle outside the half-open door. Machines beep, a refrain that soothes until a fluctuation is detected, and caterwauls ensue. Then: nurses call for doctors, chests crackle with sobs, twisted mouths amplify shouts. I avert my eyes from the redness darkening an ocher blanket on a gurney rushed down the corridor and glance at my sister—*this is not yet our fate.* I cling to my novel, a place of my own making. Its main protagonist is a cheerful nine-year-old boy. Confronted with the disappearances of his friends, he spins a story to persuade himself he is invincible. Still, he remains only a hair's breadth from vanishing. All things in his world are impermanent. From his narrative I hope to extract a truth about life that may well be about death, or perhaps what I wish to locate in his story is the possibility that as the earth cleaves under our feet, we may not always implode.

## 2.

Lying on her raised hospital bed, my sister sends me messages even though we are in the same room. *I wish I could run away. I'm fed up. Why is this happening?* The diagnosis says *terminal.* To my sister's oncologist I say, *her son is only eight.* The doctor's expression remains the same, no matter how plaintive my tone or how brightly or dimly lesions light up on her scans. He's a wiry man, a marathon runner who wears thick glasses. *Everything,* he tells us, *is in the hands of God.* When we were children, my mother would say that our family was *cursed* and, in private, my sister and I would snort at these theatrical declarations. We were arrogant then, innocent too, unfamiliar with the frailties of our bodies. Now one of the open tabs on my laptop is a prayer to St. Jude, *the patron saint of hopeless causes and desperate situations*. From bottles stamped "hazardous," chemotherapy trickles into my sister's veins through a plastic-and-silicone port a surgeon has placed by her collarbone. To write in these conditions feels like madness, feels like an act of defiance, feels like a *hopeless and desperate* attempt to find stillness between gusts of wind that will return to tear the coconut frond from the tree. My characters, once mere acquaintances, sit with me, keeping watch. Their search for truth is circuitous, incomplete. Truth shapeshifts like the spirits that haunt their dreams and warp my sentences. Alt-tab: St. Jude's prayer. Alt-tab: breakthrough in metastatic cancer treatment. Alt-tab: child narrators in literature.

## 3.

A friend says: *everything will be all right, stay positive*. Another texts, *I'm devastated*. These banalities belong to a world from which I'm now excluded. Made ruthless by grief, I delete, mute, block. I have to pick up something from a neighbor's house, and I disassemble, in envy, at the ordinariness of their day. Every four hours my sister has to swallow a morphine pill. When her pain goes down to five, or four, on a scale of one to ten, I take my laptop out of its ragged sleeve and write my novel. I'm full of rage. I can't speak to others; I can barely look at them. The only conversation I can have is with my characters. A disembodied version of me follows them as they navigate dark alleys, fear and smog burning the back of their throats. Every few seconds, my grief seeps into their skin.

**4.**

On the conditions that impede the creation of art, Virginia Woolf writes in *A Room of One's Own*, "Dogs will bark; people will interrupt; money must be made; health will break down." What was the form of the breakdown in health she imagined when she wrote those words? It must include the unraveling of the mind, but what of the physicality of grief, the distortions in the vision, the perpetual hollowness displaced occasionally by the weight of the heart that feels as if it has been recast in iron and yet beats twice as fast? What about the static current of guilt that collects at my fingertips and singes every word I type? Always the material circumstances were against me. Now the circumstances are impossible. A countdown timer like an afterimage is imprinted on my retina. Is this the right moment to say, *Let me tell you a story*?

**5.**

Nevertheless, here is a story. I am six or maybe seven and standing by a river I recognize from the poems I have read in my mother tongue. My parents have brought me along to perform the last rituals for a distant relative whose face I can't summon to my mind. The priest is brisk as he chants verses—other mourners await with red eyes, offerings, and promisingly stout wallets. Sunlight stabs the river in quick, silvery flashes. Though the meaning of the ceremony eludes me and the day is so bright as to erase even the faintest suggestion of darkness, I am aware these hours have a significance that lies just outside my grasp. At home in the evening, I tear out a page from a school notebook and write about the journey to the river, its white sands curlicued with pink, and our slight and hardy bones burnt to ash and poured into a clay pot. Then I crumple the sheet and tuck it below a sofa cushion where I believe it will escape the scrutiny of the extended family with whom we live—cousins, uncles, aunts, grandparents, a great-grandmother. A week passes, or two. I forget the river and the death. Then I find the creased page being passed around by my grandmother, who has recognized my handwriting. *It's written in English,* she says, her voice bright with what I consider to be misplaced pride. *I copied it from somewhere,* I say quickly. Already I have learned to be ashamed of my writing the same way I am of the shape of my nose and the unruliness of my hair. I have heard it said that people who want to be writers will be condemned to a life of destitution, and this condition of poverty isn't so remote to me that it's formless, like air. At school a girl I thought was my friend asks, *why does your father stay at his mother-in-law's house?* In Hindi, the language my father teaches students at a college in town, there's an impolite term for husbands who move into their wives' homes, but my parents are merely trying to save money to buy a house of their own while also living close to their children's school. My grandmother asks me, *how will you write if you're starving?* and I accept the question for what it is. In my family, awkward expressions of concern replace declarations of love. One day I will have a stable vocation, and this will ease the constraints on my imagination. Until the conditions become ideal, or at least tolerable, my writing will be my secret, not to be spilled under cushions or sometimes even on paper.

## 6.

I am twenty-one, and the words I write pay for a hostel room I share with a woman whose name I never learn and a sparrow that builds a nest on the windowsill. A clothesline runs above my bed. For my clothes to dry, I have to sleep on a damp mattress. When I'm short of money I buy a packet of cheese triangles and eat them two at a time for breakfast, lunch, and dinner. During our weekly phone conversations, I don't mention these small discomforts to my family, mindful I mustn't cause them to worry. Less altruistically, I don't want to hear—yet again—that I could have been a doctor or an accountant if only I had tried. Even though I'm writing, all my words are facts. I'm a journalist, and my shadow mustn't smudge my sentences. A man who hires me as a reporter asks if I'll get married and have children. He warns me no allowances will be made because I'm a woman. On night shifts I call the police and fire departments and sometimes write brief news articles about construction workers trapped inside collapsed buildings and mafia members killed in what the police call *encounters*. Sometimes I miss the last train and wait for dawn in a quiet office, typing up the beginnings of a novel scribbled in my reporter's notebook. It's my first attempt at writing fiction as an adult, and the words are as insubstantial as newsprint dissipating in the rain. I circle the same three chapters. I bury and excavate the same words. English is my third—or is it fourth?— language. My grandmother coaxed me into learning what was once the colonizer's tongue because she believed wealth and power spoke, and understood, only English. But in a language still alien to me I sound dishonest. Or it's not a lack of vocabulary but a lack of craft or a lack of time. All day I write down the words of others and, after my work is done, I hear their voices and see their faces—the child who lost his textbooks in a fire that engulfed an impoverished settlement or the emaciated patient at a tuberculosis hospital and the nurses who care for him without masks or gloves. Against this clamor my characters can't, or won't, make themselves heard.

7.

My grandmother falls ill and becomes confined to her bed. When I visit she asks me for something to read and carelessly I lend her a book I have just purchased from a bookstore in my hometown. After she dies I pick up the novel, tracing with my fingertips the sentences on the pages as she must have. From disuse I have lost my fluency in my mother tongue and letters don't coalesce into words as quickly as they once did. In the novel an elderly woman finds pleasure in food as her life becomes confined to her room, but as death approaches, she starves herself. Made fragile by weakening bones, my grandmother too corresponded with the outside world through food, but in those last few weeks when I left the novel with her, she began to refuse to eat. Did life follow art, or did art merely illustrate the machinery of death as others had witnessed before? I can't shake off the feeling that I gave my grandmother a manual for dying. I abandon my novel, seeking her forgiveness, or approval, too late.

8.

After years as a journalist I uproot myself from my country to follow my husband to England. What ought to have been an impossible decision is made easier by a mysterious illness that makes it difficult for me to work. I can no longer sleep. Acid coats my tongue. Flames reach up from my gut to scald my mouth. Under a gray English sky, I shuffle to the local surgery and find it has a mercurial roster of GPs. I never meet the same doctor twice, but individually they conclude my illness is only in my mind. A few suggest antidepressants. Perhaps I'm depressed. I'm unemployed. A cousin has died of cancer, the same disease her mother had; she was too young to die. I grieve for her, but selfishly I also grieve for myself, the life I once believed I could pursue at forty, sixty, eighty. Encoded in my genes too may be an error, a glitch, a misprint. There's no certainty I'll reach the age my grandmother was when she died. With this realization arrives a second one: even as I discarded stories and novels, I had hoped to complete them one day. Since childhood I had been waiting for *one day* when I would become the person I wanted to be—self-assured, stable-incomed, secure about my accent and the way in which I had made English mine, a writer with the perfect word to describe inscrutable expressions, the rains, the polluted skies. But *one day* is a myth. Time is finite. In this moment, I must be myself and also the version of me I would have been at forty or sixty or eighty. I begin another novel.

**9.**

My illness has a name: intestinal tuberculosis. A "third-world" disease that hid itself in my gut so slyly that doctors didn't detect it for years. Perhaps the illness wasn't cunning in its disguise; perhaps the doctors dismissed me too easily. I'm brown-skinned, female, an immigrant who can't get the smell of *curry* out of my coat even if I open all the windows in my flat as I cook, never accounting for the seasons. Snow on the pavement. Turmeric stains on my palms. I speak softly. When I type on my laptop I always have a finger on the delete key. I'm diffident, inchoate, yet determined I have something to say. But desire isn't equivalent to skill. I test the techniques I learned in the short courses I have taken in creative writing since moving to the new country, the metropole. *Summarize your scenes. Draw a narrative arc. Interview your characters.* The list of twenty questions I'm meant to ask protagonists include *do you prefer showers or baths?* My characters are unfamiliar with bathtubs; they don't open taps with the expectation that water will gush out. Every question, however quotidian, magnifies the difference that I and my writing embody. The inhabitants of my novel seek shade, not sun. They linger and digress with no consideration for pace. Their language, their imagery, is ornate and obscure. When they serenade their lovers, they sing, *you're my liver,* not *you're my heart.* To write like my peers in a Western classroom I have to erase myself, but if I erase myself I have no story. This is complicated by my secret wish to be someone else. I'm taking sixteen pills a day, and the antibiotics turn my tears an orangish red. Waiting to see doctors, nurses, or pharmacists at the hospital, my body altered by the disease and its cure such that it's unrecognizable to myself, I write my novel in a notebook. If I look closely at the page, in between the slanting rows of sentences, I may catch a glimpse of my former self.

## 10.

I complete my treatment. I finish my novel too, but it's swiftly rejected. I despair, for months. The upside is that I can now cry without red trails on my cheeks. I don't write for a while, but eventually my desire to tell a story exceeds my fear that it's not worth telling. If to write is to transgress, then alongside the unease of transgression flickers a thrill that provokes and compels. But: the passage of time is quick and reliable, and my writing is slow and capricious. I decide to expunge all else from my life—the copywriting and copyediting and retail jobs I have been taking on to pay the bills—and spend a year studying for a master's degree in creative writing. But first I'm required to pass a test to prove I'm proficient in English. The university won't waive this requirement despite my years as a journalist for English newspapers in India and the short stories I have published in England. Self-conscious, humiliated, I take a standardized English language test and become voluble in the "Speaking" component of the exam. When the examiner asks an innocuous question about my life in England, I respond with anecdotes about teenagers on skateboards shouting *Go home stinky Paki* and shopkeepers pulling the sleeves of their cardigans down to their fingertips and refusing to serve me. I pass the test. The university offers me a place in the master's program, but not a scholarship. I cash out pensions and empty my savings to pay the tuition and living fees. It's an act of faith by an unbeliever. So many bad things have happened in my life, I figure the universe owes me a good turn.

## 11.

In truth I'm not counting on the benevolence of the universe but its "indifference," which Woolf describes as "notorious" and James Baldwin as "frightening." To me, indifference will be a blessing.

## 12.

My husband loses his job a month after I accept a place on the master's program. Our circumstances are such that a year in which neither of us earns money is untenable. I switch to studying part-time so that I can work. My husband finds another job, but it seems the universe, a higher power, a belligerent ancestral spirit, the curse my mother warned us about, whatever I choose to call it, wants me to stop writing, and it's not asking this of me with tact or grace. It's a trope in horror films that the frightened character will leave their place of safety to investigate the source of their disquiet, always to their detriment. On the train to the university, I wonder if I'm this character. Outside the window the scenery is serene: rolling green hills, bales of hay scattered across yellow fields, the occasional bright red face of a pheasant. Perhaps it's not the universe I fear but the absurdity of my enterprise. In the classroom I can't hide my writing. I'll be exposed, and it will be a relief to know I'm not a writer. Then I'll be forced to find another way to be in the world.

## 13.

Chekhov, Conrad, Kafka: the gods at the university are white (and often consumptive, though only I seem to be attentive to this fact). Mythology is mostly Greek. I workshop the beginning of my second novel, and a tutor suggests I rewrite it from the perspective of a character who doesn't exist on the page. I shelve the novel, whose first draft I managed to complete before the course began, in between my retail and copyediting jobs, waking up to write when the sky was still black until the sun lightened the east. Acquaintances ask how I'm faring in a classroom with those half my age. Aren't prodigies twenty-five at most? *I need weeks to write what takes the young people hours,* I tell someone I met on a short writing course. *Were you born with what most of them have?* she asks. It's only then that I truly appreciate the workings of privilege. Where I grew up, we learned to cover our chests with textbooks and walked with our heads bowed, afraid of the glances of strangers, especially men. Where I live now I wear the drabbest of clothes, unwilling to stand out and risk more hostility than what the color of my skin already evokes. Is it any surprise then that there's always a gap—an abyss, really—between what I want to say and how I say it?

## 14.

My mother whispers in a phone call that my favorite uncle doesn't have backache, as she had told me earlier. He has cancer, he's dying, he's dead. In his house I can barely breathe because guilt is a stone in my throat, its edges sharper than his absence. I didn't witness his pain; I arrived too late; I was writing my second novel which has since been shoved into a folder named *never-want-to-see-again-files*. Having no recourse to prayer, I turn to the laws of probability I was taught in a statistics class decades ago. Perhaps an equation—solid, neat, precise—can suggest the likelihood of this unexpected outcome, a life enfolded by loss. But my maths is rusty, or this is a ledger that can't be balanced. If I were to read the story of my family in a novel, would I not consider the litany of adversities that has befallen us implausible? The function of the poet, Aristotle writes, is to depict *what is possible according to the law of probability or necessity.*

*Everything irrational,* he says, *should be excluded.* If I go by these tenets I will have to infer that the entire narrative of my life is irrational, and what then will it say about my writing, which is no more separate from me than my breath? Contorted by grief, objects blur, collapse, collide in my vision, and still I notice my sister leans to the left as she walks. A vicious pain flares down her left arm and shoulder and sometimes around her ribs. Doctors ask for X-rays and MRIs of the spine and, finding nothing suspicious, prescribe yoga and swimming, walks, and vitamin D. *Be happy, you don't have cancer,* one of the thirteen doctors she sees says, scrolling through her thoracic MRI images on his computer screen. No twists in this tale: you already know what happens next.

## 15.

The ghost of my grandmother speaks to me. The words are scornful, which is unlike her, so it must be the echo of my own voice that I hear: *Why write? Will your writing cure cancer?* Splintered by sorrow, faces lined by shock, my parents tend to my sister. They say nothing to me but seem bewildered by the deplorable chatter of my laptop keys. My behavior is unacceptable, even to myself. In the face of persistent misfortune, the appropriate response would be to disintegrate or malfunction. What I can't explain: to shape a story on the page is to forestall, or at the very least pause, the fragmentation of the self. "You have to do your work," the unnamed male writer in Kathryn Chetkovich's essay "Envy" tells her. "That's your first responsibility." For years I had this quote tacked to my laptop, an incantation to begin the day, but one uttered without belief. Writing is an abstraction, unlike a career, or children. Having neither, even a doctor suggests I should be my sister's caregiver. When I think of women who don't have children or incomes, their backs appear slightly hunched from stooping over woodfires and stoves. Their cracked, sooty fingers massage aches out of weary feet and braid rebellious hair. I knew these women in my childhood; I remember the grace in their hands. Who am I to deny the expectations placed on me on account of my gender, culture, and race and say this honest work isn't my calling? The days are hot and bright, but the hospital room is dark and we sit under fluorescent lights whose glare injudiciously reveals every turn of the mouth, every nervous tap of the finger. I wait for my characters to have an epiphany that hasn't occurred to me yet.

## 16.

It's Christmas break. I don't travel home as planned, and instead edit my novel. It has been accepted for publication. At 3 A.M. the phone beeps with my sister's scan results. Another treatment has failed; the failure is mine. I have abandoned my family to write. I go to a therapist. A Freudian with voluminous hair, she takes copious notes. Still, by the third session, she has forgotten parts of what I told her. She glances at her notepad and insists, *I would have remembered if you had mentioned it before.* I don't return, but I suspect the truth is that no one can keep track of the convolutions of my story, not even me. It's protracted, misshapen, rough. Spatially or temporally it can't be confined to a single space or moment. Of such stories a tutor once said *simplify, simplify, simplify. If there are multiple time shifts, make sure the story is rooted to one setting. Give the reader a stable focal point.* Neither in storytelling nor in life can I follow these directions. In my dreams it's summer and I am with my sister and I wake up and it's a winter night in England and the darkness is silent, a kind of silence I have never known in India, where as I tried to sleep I would hear crickets, frogs, dogs, ceiling fans, trucks, cars, and on two occasions, the guttural roars of shifting tectonic plates.

## 17.

The serenity prayer, rephrased: I accept that in my life I will never have the ideal conditions for writing. Still, I click on websites of residencies to which I can't apply, and the cursor hovers above photographs of charming cabins in the woods or by a blue lake. I believe that the writers at these residencies go to sleep, and wake up, with their characters entangled in their dreams. I worry the distance between my life and that of my characters is too much and also too little. In the period before publication but after the second round of edits I hear from my publishers that my novel is *too sad. It will make for a terrible Christmas present. It won't sell.* If I make the story hopeful, it may minimize the discomfort the white reader feels. The Indian reader won't accuse me of *selling out*, of dressing up our trauma and poverty for western consumption. I think of the therapist who flicked through my inventory of tragedies and couldn't name it afterward. Why would the hypothetical reader be any different? I should abridge the narrative, stitch it neatly so that its seams won't come undone, grant it a coherence my life itself lacks. I should spin distress into something pretty and palatable and soft. But this is not the life I know. However far I travel, it seems I can't dislodge the red earth of home under my nails.

18.

*This writer can't perform happiness. Reader discretion is advised.*

19.

I wish my wavering voice would become a memory. But even after the publication of my novel I remain hesitant. Now when I write, I hear the grievances of readers, some of whom obligingly emailed me, or tagged me on social media, to say my writing has too many *Indian* words, the action is slow, the narrative is digressive and disheartening. These are imperfect conditions for writing. My conversations with my characters should be private. I must strive for silence. I must be tenacious. The difficulty is that I can't separate art from life. To write I must access my fears and joys and shame but not to the extent that it subsumes the fictionality of the world I have created. Sometimes I manage to reach that state of transcendence where only the characters are real, and then I'm pulled out of that moment by the humdrum of existential dread. In "That to Study Philosophy is to Learn to Die," Michel de Montaigne writes, ". . . and then let death take me planting my cabbages, indifferent to him, and still less of my gardens not being finished." I have begun to think of my writing as a garden of vegetables. It suits me, the earthiness of this image. Today I must remain content with the words I have written and be indifferent to the mud encrusting the hems of my trousers, the moth holes in the fabric of the story, and the caterpillars burrowing toward the heart of the narrative.

20.

In England, seagulls congregate above a car park I can see from my
window. Even on days when there's a yellow warning for strong
wind, they shriek, grunt, and fly in loops for what seems like hours,
their wings refusing to bend to the will of nature. They have forsaken
cliffs for concrete, sand for tarmac. An article on the BBC website
calls the birds "*urban.*" In the weeks following the publication of my
novel, when a lockdown is enforced and the landscape is silent except for the sound of sirens, I watch the gulls, who like me are—or
are pretending to be—at home in an unnatural habitat. To choose to
write in a life like mine seems as ill advised as deciding to fly in a
storm. But I can hope that it has by now become involuntary, like
breathing, or a habit, the way I look to the right and left before I cross
the road. For some in my extended family I'm a cautionary tale to
warn children at risk of slipping into unconventionality. I'm the bo-
geyman, the monster under the bed, the writer. My sister is dead and
I'm writing another novel. "But you did that already," a relative says
when we return to my parents' house after performing my sister's
last rites by the river. She is ashes and bones in the pot I hold and the
pink crying baby in a hospital cot whose pinched face I can see only
by standing on tiptoe. I'm in a future I didn't imagine for her, or for
me. I should be inconsolable, but I'm writing.

21.

I want this text to be a rallying cry, a pledge, a placeholder for hope,
an anthem, an answer. But it's none of these things. My truth is

mine alone, and malleable. Today we may grieve by wailing or writing and tomorrow by numbing our fractured minds—who can tell us how we must commune with our ghosts and demons or if our words ought to be soft or shrill? Once you calibrate the breadth of your life to make space for uncertainty, words refuse to assume the form of instructions. I cannot conjure an aphorism that will comfort or console. For long periods in my life I didn't write because I thought I couldn't, I mustn't; because I was a girl, poor, ill, brown; because I was without skill, language, time. I walked with words tucked beneath my tongue, afraid to release them to the air. I expected a constellation of good omens. I expected a voice, firm and certain, to tell me that *now* it was time for me to write. I expected a stilling. These were false expectations. I waited for the circumstances to change, for the impediments to my writing to evaporate like speckles of sweat, or fade like bruises. I looked to writing for meaning, but then in the act of writing a key turned, and I entered a room from where I saw that fiction was a mirror that contained the fractiousness of the landscape, whittling or refracting the startling incandescence of that which I couldn't bear to look in the eye. How the world receives my work, I can no more alter than I can disarrange the veins of a leaf or the trajectory of the sun. If I still speak to my characters every day, wear their clothes, wince at the cuts in their flesh or the pebbles grazing their feet through the holes in their slippers, it's because through them I may find my bearings or reach a place where fear and shame are as valid as happiness and hope. It's a sliver of a miracle, a small gift. I wish this for you.

## Reading Suggestions

James Baldwin, *Collected Essays*, edited by Toni Morrison

Michel de Montaigne, *Essays*

Paul Kalanithi, *When Breath Becomes Air*

Tishani Doshi, *Girls Are Coming Out of the Woods*

Diana Khoi Nguyen, *Ghost Of*

Anne Carson, *Nox*

Christopher Reid, *A Scattering*

V. S. Naipaul, *A House for Mr. Biswas*

Akhil Sharma, *Family Life*

# Acknowledgments

The editors would like to thank: Caitlin McKenna, Alex Russell, Noa Shapiro, Charlotte Humphery, Matthew Turner, Natasha Fairweather, Peter Straus, Avani Shah, Radha Smith, Neon Yang, Kristien Potgieter, CJ Fiala, and the organizers of the Bread Loaf Writers' Conferences.

# Contributors

**LEILA ABOULELA** is the author of five novels: *Bird Summons, The Translator* (a *New York Times* 100 Notable Books of the Year), *The Kindness of Enemies, Minaret,* and *Lyrics Alley* (Fiction Winner of the Scottish Book Awards). She was the first winner of the Caine Prize for African Writing in 2000, and her latest story collection, *Elsewhere, Home,* won the Saltire Fiction Book of the Year Award. Leila's work has been translated into fifteen languages, and she was longlisted three times for the Orange Prize (now the Women's Prize for Fiction). Her plays *The Insider, The Mystic Life,* and others were broadcast on BBC Radio and her fiction included in publications such as *Freeman's, Granta,* and *Harper's.* Leila is honorary president of the Society for the Study of the Sudans UK (SSSUK) and a trustee of Jalada Africa, a Pan-African writers' collective. Her sixth novel, *River Spirit,* is due for publication in 2023.

**TAHMIMA ANAM'S** first novel, *A Golden Age,* won the Commonwealth Writers Prize and went on to be translated into twenty-seven languages. It was followed by *The Good Muslim* and *The Bones of Grace.* She is the recipient of the O. Henry Award and has been named one of the "Best Young British Novelists" by *Granta*. Born in Dhaka, Bangladesh, she trained as a social anthropologist at Harvard University and works at a tech company, an experience that formed the basis of her latest novel, *The Startup Wife* (Scribner, 2021).

**VIDA CRUZ-BORJA** is a Filipina fantasy and science fiction writer, editor, artist, and conrunner. "On the Inactive Protagonist" won the 2022 IGNYTE Award for Best Creative Nonfiction. Her short fiction and essays have been published or are forthcoming from *The Magazine of Fantasy and Science Fiction, Fantasy Magazine, Strange Horizons, PodCastle, Expanded Horizons*, and various anthologies. Her work has been nominated, longlisted, and recommended for the Hugo Award, the British Science Fiction Award, and the James Tiptree Jr. (now Otherwise) Award. She is a Clarion 2014 alumna and the author of two illustrated short story collections: *Beyond the Line of Trees* (2019) and *Song of the Mango and Other New Myths* (2022). Currently, she is a freelance book editor with Tessera Editorial and The Darling Axe and is co-director of BonFIYAH under the larger umbrella of FIYAHCON, a BIPOC-centered convention for science fiction and fantasy readers and writers.

**XIAOLU GUO** is an award-winning Chinese British novelist, essayist, and filmmaker. Her novels include *A Concise Chinese-English Dictionary for Lovers* (Orange Prize Shortlist 2007), *Village of Stone*, and *I Am China* (a 2014 NPR's Best Book). Her memoir *Once Upon a Time in the East* won the National Book Critics Circle Award 2017 and was shortlisted for the Royal Society of Literature Award. It was also a *Sunday Times* Book of the Year. Her novel *A Lover's Discourse* was shortlisted for the Goldsmith Prize 2020 and longlisted for the Orwell Prize 2021. She has also directed a dozen films, including *How Is Your Fish Today?* (Sundance Official Selection 2007), which won the Grand Jury Prize at the International Women's Film Festival, France. *UFO in Her Eyes* premiered at Toronto (TIFF 2010) and was produced by the renowned German-Turkish filmmaker Fatih Akin. Her feature *She, a Chinese* received the Golden Leopard Award at the Locarno Film Festival 2009. Her documentaries include *We Went to Wonderland* (premiered at the MoMA in New York 2008), *Once Upon a Time Proletarian* (Venice Film Festival 2009), and *Five Men and a Caravaggio* (BFI London Film Festival 2018). Her most recent book is *Radical*, to be published in 2023. She is currently a visiting professor at the Free University in Berlin.

**MYRIAM GURBA** is a writer and activist living in Long Beach, California. She is the author of several books, including *Mean*, an experimental memoir. Her essays have appeared in *The New York Times, The Los Angeles Times, The Paris Review, Harper's Bazaar,* and *The Believer.* She is a co-founder of Dignidad Literaria, a social movement that combats white supremacy in publishing.

**MOHAMMED HANIF** is a journalist and novelist based in Karachi. He is the author of three novels: *A Case of Exploding Mangoes, Our Lady of Alice Bhatti,* and *Red Birds.* He has also written a pamphlet for the Human Rights Commission of Pakistan titled "The Baloch Who Is Not Missing, and Others Who Are." As a journalist he was the head of BBC's Urdu Service and now writes for *The New York Times, The Guardian, Dawn,* BBC Urdu, and BBC Punjabi.

**ZEYN JOUKHADAR** is the author of the novels *The Thirty Names of Night*, which won the Lambda Literary Award and the Stonewall Book Award, and *The Map of Salt and Stars*, which won the Middle East Book Award, was a Goodreads Choice Awards and Wilbur Smith Adventure Writing Prize finalist, and has been translated into more than a dozen languages. His work has appeared in the *Kink* anthology, *Salon*, *The Paris Review*, *[PANK]*, and elsewhere and has been twice nominated for the Pushcart Prize. Joukhadar guest-edited *Mizna*'s 2020 Queer + Trans Voices issue, serves on the board of the Radius of Arab American Writers (RAWI), and mentors emerging writers of color with the Periplus Collective.

**FEMI KAYODE** grew up in Lagos, Nigeria. He studied psychology at the University of Ibadan and has worked in advertising over the last two decades. He was a Packard Fellow in Film and Media at the University of Southern California and a Gates-Packard Fellow in International Health at the University of Washington, Seattle. His writing credits include several award-winning works for the stage and screen. He holds an MA in Creative Writing–Crime Fiction from the University of East Anglia, where *Lightseekers* won the Little, Brown/UEA Crime Fiction Award and went on to be longlisted for the Gold Dagger 2022. He is currently pursuing a PhD in Crime Fiction at Bath Spa University, where he is expounding on the use of Systems Thinking for plotting the contemporary crime novel. He lives in Namibia with his family.

**JAMIL JAN KOCHAI** is the author of *99 Nights in Logar* (Viking, 2019), a finalist for the Pen/Hemingway Award for Debut Novel and the DSC Prize for South Asian Literature. He was born in an Afghan refugee camp in Peshawar, Pakistan, but he originally hails from Logar, Afghanistan. His short stories have appeared in *The New Yorker, Ploughshares, The O. Henry Prize Stories,* and *The Best American Short Stories.* Currently, he is a Stegner Fellow at Stanford University. His second book *The Haunting of Hajji Hotak and Other Stories* was published by Viking in 2022.

**AMITAVA KUMAR** is the author of several works of fiction and nonfiction. His writings have appeared in *Granta, Harper's, The New York Times, Caravan,* and other publications. Recently, he published *The Blue Book: A Writer's Journal* containing his drawings and diary entries made during the pandemic. Kumar has been awarded a Guggenheim Fellowship and residencies at Yaddo, MacDowell, the Lannan Foundation, and the Rockefeller Foundation at Bellagio. His novel *Immigrant, Montana* was on the best of the year lists at *The New Yorker* and *The New York Times* as well as President Barack Obama's list of favorite books of 2018. His new novel *A Time Outside This Time* was described by *The New Yorker* as "a shimmering assault on the Zeitgeist." Kumar is also the author of a book on writing and style entitled *Every Day I Write the Book.* He teaches at Vassar College in upstate New York. More at amitavakumar.com.

**KIESE LAYMON** is a Black southern writer from Jackson, Mississippi. Laymon is the author of the genre-bending novel *Long Division,* and the essay collection *How to Slowly Kill Yourself and Others in America.* Laymon's bestselling memoir, *Heavy: An American Memoir,* won the 2019 Andrew Carnegie Medal for Excellence in Nonfiction, the 2018 Christopher Isherwood Prize for Autobiographical Prose, and the Austen Riggs Erikson Prize for Excellence in Mental Health Media, and was named one of the 50 Best Memoirs of the Past 50 Years by *The New York Times*. The audiobook, read by the author, was named the Audible 2018 Audiobook of the Year. He is the recipient of a 2020–2021 Radcliffe Fellowship at Harvard. He is at work on several new projects, including the long poem *Good God,* the horror comedy *And So On*, the children's book *City Summer, Country Summer,* and the film *Heavy: An American Memoir.* He is the founder of the Catherine Coleman Literary Arts and Justice Initiative, a program aimed at getting Mississippi kids and their parents more comfortable reading, writing, revising, and sharing.

**NADIFA MOHAMED** was born in Somalia and raised in the United Kingdom. She holds a degree from Oxford University in history and politics. Her first novel, *Black Mamba Boy,* was based on her father's childhood experiences in East Africa and the Middle East. It won the Betty Trask Prize; was shortlisted for the Guardian First Book Prize, the John Llewellyn Rhys Prize, the Dylan Thomas Prize, and the PEN Open Book Award; and was longlisted for the Orange Prize. Her second novel, *The Orchard of Lost Souls,* is set in Somalia during the Siyad Barre dictatorship; it won the Somerset Maugham Award and the Prix Albert Bernard. It was shortlisted for the Hurston/Wright Legacy Award and longlisted for the Dylan Thomas Award. Nadifa Mohamed's novels have been translated into twenty languages, and in 2013 she was selected as one of *Granta*'s "Best of Young British Novelists," a once-in-a-decade honor. Her new novel, *The Fortune Men,* was published by Viking UK and was a finalist for the Booker Prize and the Costa Book Award 2021.

**INGRID ROJAS CONTRERAS** was born and raised in Bogotá, Colombia. Her debut novel *Fruit of the Drunken Tree* was the silver medal winner in First Fiction from the California Book Awards and a *New York Times* editor's choice. Her essays and short stories have appeared in *The New York Times Magazine, The Cut,* and ZYZZYVA, among others. *The Man Who Could Move Clouds,* a true family story about her mestizo curandero grandfather, is her first memoir and was published by Doubleday in 2022. She lives in California.

**SHARLENE TEO'S** debut novel, *Ponti,* won the inaugural Deborah Rogers Writer's Award. Her writing has appeared in anthologies such as *East Side Voices* and *At the Pond* and in publications such as *Granta, McSweeney's,* and *The Guardian.*

**MADELEINE THIEN** is the author of four books of fiction, including *Dogs at the Perimeter* and *Do Not Say We Have Nothing,* which focused on art, politics, and revolution, most notably in Cambodia and China. Her work has been shortlisted for the Booker Prize, Women's Prize for Fiction, and the Folio Prize; longlisted for a Carnegie Medal; and translated into more than twenty-five languages. She has received Canada's two highest literary honors, the Giller Prize and the Governor-General's Literary Award for Fiction. Her essays and stories have appeared in *The New Yorker, Granta, The New York Review of Books, The Guardian, Brick,* and elsewhere. She teaches writing and literature at the City University of New York and lives between Brooklyn and Montreal.

**TIPHANIE YANIQUE** is the author of the novel *Monster in the Middle,* which was published in 2021, was a finalist for the Lambda

Literary Awards, and was included on numerous best of the year lists. Tiphanie is also the author of the poetry collection *Wife*, which won the Bocas Prize in Caribbean poetry and the United Kingdom's Forward/Felix Dennis Prize for a First Collection; and the novel *Land of Love and Drowning*, which won the Flaherty-Dunnan First Novel Award from the Center for Fiction, the Phillis Wheatley Award for Pan-African Literature, and the American Academy of Arts and Letters Rosenthal Family Foundation Award. *Land of Love and Drowning* was also a finalist for the Orion Award in Environmental Literature and the Hurston-Wright Legacy Award. She is the author of a collection of stories, *How to Escape from a Leper Colony*, which won her a listing as one of the National Book Foundation's "5 Under 35" and the Bocas Prize in Fiction. Her writing has won the Boston Review Prize in Fiction, the Rona Jaffe Foundation Writers Award, the Pushcart Prize, a Fulbright Scholarship, and the Academy of American Poets Prize. Tiphanie is from the Virgin Islands and is an associate professor at Emory University.

**DEEPA ANAPPARA** was born in Kerala, South India. Her first novel, *Djinn Patrol on the Purple Line*, won the Edgar Award for Best Novel, was longlisted for the Women's Prize for Fiction, and was shortlisted for the JCB Prize for Indian Literature. It was named one of the best books of 2020 by *The New York Times*, *The Washington Post*, *Time*, and NPR and is currently being translated into twenty-three languages. She previously worked as a journalist in India, and her reports on the impact of poverty and religious violence on children won the Developing Asia Journalism Awards, the Every Human Has Rights Media Awards, and the Sanskriti-Prabha Dutt Fellowship in Journalism.

**TAYMOUR SOOMRO** was born in Lahore, Pakistan. He read law at Cambridge University and Stanford Law School. He has worked as a corporate solicitor in London and Milan, a lecturer at a university in Karachi, an agricultural estate manager in rural Sindh, and a publicist for a luxury fashion brand in London. He has published a textbook on law with Oxford University Press and has written for Pakistani news outlets. His short story "Philosophy of the Foot" appeared in *The New Yorker* in January 2019. His short fiction has since been published in *Ninth Letter* and *The Southern Review*. His debut novel, *Other Names for Love,* was published by Farrar, Straus and Giroux (U.S.) and Harvill Secker (U.K.) in July 2022. He is currently a fellow at the Wisconsin Institute for Creative Writing.